Evolutionary Groups: A New Frontier in Human Connection

As your groups awaken, so do you

Patricia Pfost and Anne Altvater

ISBN: 979-8-9999852-0-0

Cover and text design by Hello Lovely Design and Co hellolovely.design

Cover image by Fahri, Adobe Stock

First Edition

10 9 8 7 6 5 4 3 2 1

Dedication

I am feeling great gratitude for this group that keeps reminding us of who we are, reminding me of who I am, so I can be more fully Us.

Evolutionary Groups course participant

This book is dedicated to the Us of all of us.

Contents

PART III: The Eight Elements That Move Any Group Toward Unity Consciousness

PART IV: Integration, Practice, and Conclusion

APPENDICES

Preface

We are entering an era of a new quality of group awareness. Even in how we name authorship, we begin to reorient the way we think about groups—not as hierarchical clusters of individuals, but as living intelligent fields that can cohere, awaken, and evolve.

The origin of this guidebook is collective. It arose from the group being of the New Wave of Groups founders, Anne and Patricia, and the participants in our courses and gatherings who have evolved this work over the past seven years. Not one of us could have done it without all of us, and together we are amazing!

Each of us plays a role. Some are the receiving ear. Some are the vessel, the voice, the translator. Others hold the frequency, ask the precise question, or quietly anchor the space. These roles aren't assigned. They arise naturally from our longings and our gifts. And when we meet in presence and mutual regard, something greater moves among us. We bring each other forth. Voilà—a creation is born not from any one person alone, but from the shared field that arises as our being together.

The material and perspectives offered here arise from decades of experience in groups, teachings, and personal inquiry. We don't claim scientific authority. What we offer is a lived lens—shaped by what we've witnessed, sensed, and become in the field of human connection. May it serve as a doorway into your own unfolding awareness.

PART I

Foundations: A New Frontier in Human Connection

The real voyage of discovery consists not in seeking new landscapes, but in having new eyes.
— *Marcel Proust, Remembrance of Things Past*

Welcome

You don't need to be an expert in group facilitation to sense that something more is possible when people come together.

Maybe you've led work teams or sat in family meetings, wishing for more honesty, ease, or connection. Maybe you've gathered with friends, clients, or spiritual companions and touched something luminous, but couldn't explain how it happened or how to find your way back.

This guidebook is for those moments of quiet recognition, or deeper longing, when something within you whispers, "There's more here."

Whether you're looking for practical tools to make your meetings more engaging, or you're curious about the unseen energies that move through your groups, here you will find ways to explore both.

Come enter this evolutionary territory with us and begin to sense the presence—the being—of your New Wave groups. To begin, all you need is curiosity and a willingness to see groups as living possibilities.

What Is a Group?

We define a group simply as two or more who are gathered with any purpose in mind.

When meeting with colleagues, talking with your child, engaging with your pet, or navigating the many perspectives inside your head, you are in a group.

And every group has the potential to come more fully alive.

A New Quality of Group Awareness

Groups aren't new. What is new is the growing human capacity to experience them in a fundamentally different way, more than simply collections of individuals or channels for communication, but as living and conscious fields of intelligence.

This is an evolution in our perception and is supported by developments in neuroscience, psychology, systems thinking, collective intelligence research, relational and consciousness-based practices, and—perhaps most significantly—the lived experience. Across disciplines, language is emerging to describe this shift in how we are perceiving—and indeed experiencing—ourselves and others when we come together: relational fields, group minds, co-presence, co-awakening, interbeing, shared emergence, the being of the group, and many more.

We are not simply naming a field that surrounds us—we are speaking from within the shared experience we have of being a unified field with others. It's not observational; it's participatory, co-arising, and self-aware. Rather than being a "My experience," it is a "We experience."

Human beings have always longed for deeper connection, not just emotionally but existentially. Mystics, poets, and wisdom keepers across the ages have voiced this yearning, pointing toward a timeless union beyond separation.

What is becoming more visible now is a field of awareness that has always been here, waiting beneath the surface of ordinary life. Being able to see it is a next step in the unfolding of our longing. We are beginning to notice a relational presence that holds us together, a subtle atmosphere that grows stronger as we meet with honesty and attunement. Within it, we experience a shared life, intelligence moving through us as one.

What we have longed for is beginning to take form. In the circles where we gather—whether to work, create, learn, heal, play, or simply be—the qualities once glimpsed only in rare moments of grace are becoming steadily more possible.

This guidebook will help you "Look here!"

When we gather with the kind of attention invited in the following pages, we become a shared presence, not just as an idea but as a felt experience. We bring ourselves more fully to one another. We listen with a new depth. We are the flow, effortless and natural. Insights land. The group begins to function as a unified intelligence greater than the sum of its parts.

Surprisingly, in this shared presence, our individual uniqueness remains intact. We come into a sharper focus; we are more ourselves than ever, even as we are part of something greater.

And when that shift happens, we recognize it. Increasingly, we recognize when it's missing too. Meetings feel flat. Conversations lose vitality. Something essential seems just out of reach.

Yet, it doesn't take a loud voice or group consensus to begin again. It starts with one person—you—making a quiet choice to sense, turn inward, and to respond differently. From that moment, something new becomes possible.

We are standing at the edge of a perceptual turning point. Sometimes, just one subtle shift—a pause, a breath, a different kind of listening—can ripple through a group and open a new quality of space. Come with us as we explore this terrain.

Who Is This Guidebook For?

Anyone, really!

- Families and communities who want more honesty, creativity, warmth, and healing

- Individuals who feel the hidden intelligence of groups but don't always have language for it

- People who want their group experiences—at work, at home, in life—to feel more real and less like a performance

Whether your interest is deeply spiritual or quietly practical, this book is designed to meet you where you are. You can use it as a guide, a workbook, or a personal reflection journal. It will grow with you.

How This Guidebook Works

This is a book you can begin using today—with your partner at the dinner table, your coworkers in a meeting, or your friends in everyday conversation. You'll find simple practices, prompts to open exploration, and ways of speaking and listening that bring more connection, creativity, and flow into your group experiences.

You might choose to read the book from start to finish or just skim and dip into the parts that call to you for an entirely new and exciting perspective on groups. You can also open it to any page, element, or exercise, and begin right there.

Some of what's offered here is small and immediate: a shift in attention, a new kind of listening, a practice to try in your next shared moment. Other parts go deeper—re-patterning how your gatherings move, relate, and evolve.

The Evolutionary Groups model offers a fresh lens on collective life through two doorways of exploration: the Three Groups Continuum and the Eight Elements That Move Any Group Toward Unity Consciousness.

This model offers a way not only to understand the circles you are part of, but to transform them from the inside out, moment by moment.

The Three Groups Continuum describes the ways groups express themselves and how these expressions are naturally evolving. At times, our groups lean on structure and clear roles. At others, they explore new ways of listening, sensing, or collaborating. And sometimes, something entirely unexpected takes shape.

These movements aren't fixed or linear—they're the living responses of a group field to its people, purpose, and conditions. Seeing where your group is at any moment can open more possibilities for how you participate and what you invite next.

The Eight Elements That Move Any Group Toward Unity Consciousness are subtle shifts in attention and attitude that can change the atmosphere of a group and how people respond to one another. They are not steps or rules, however. They're real-time choices you can make at any moment—choices that invite more honesty in the shared space, more ease in participation, and a way of listening that lets new possibilities take shape. Each element offers a different doorway into sensing the group as a living being and engaging with it in a more aware, responsive way. Together, the elements create an environment in which the group feels more alive and able to respond to what is most needed in the moment.

What's Included in This Guidebook

Simple practices that you can use in the moment—to loosen up a conversation, shift the mood of a meeting, or bring more presence and connection to whatever group you're in.

What you might say to support you in opening space, inviting honesty, and moving conversations forward without force.

Prompts you and your group can explore together to deepen awareness of your group's dynamics—helping you notice what's actually happening beneath the surface and the new choices that are available.

Scenarios to help you recognize what's possible and feel inspired to try things in your own way.

Easy ways to sharpen your awareness, so you can sense what's really going on within a group, even when nothing is being said, and choose how to respond in a way that brings more authenticity.

Let's Begin

This guidebook asks you to notice your groups, rather than presenting ways to fix them. To respond, not react, with more choice, awareness, and care. It's not about mastering a method, either. It's about entering a deeper experience of what's possible when people come together. You can start anywhere. Every step is useful. Each line is an entry point. Every moment of noticing matters. Try one new idea. Use one prompt. Pause with one question. Even the smallest shift in perception can change everything.

The more you apply what's here, the more you will remember that you have choices, and the more coherent your groups will become, with greater ease, increased flow, optimal alignment with what really matters, and deepened unity.

PART II

The Three Groups Continuum

Life is a process of becoming, a combination
of states we have to go through.
— *Anaïs Nin, The Diary of Anaïs Nin*

How Groups Evolve and Shift, Moment by Moment

Just as we evolve, so do our groups. We work on ourselves to grow, learn, and live more fully, yet the groups we belong to also need our conscious attention if they are to thrive. Every gathering you're part of, from a family to a team to a friendship, is a living field that evolves as time progresses. The field can open, contract, stagnate, mature, or even awaken, depending on how it is met and supported.

The Three Groups Continuum—from Conventional, through Transitional, into New Wave—offers a way to notice how a group is functioning in any given moment. It's a lens for sensing what's present—what's guiding the group—and whether something else is preferable and possible. This perspective applies to all groups, even small ones: you and a friend, a partner, or just your child. The Continuum also lives within us; it can help you notice your own "inner group" of the thoughts, beliefs, and feelings that you carry inside.

The Continuum reveals how groups move through and evolve beyond familiar patterns—from separation into connection, from externally defined roles to internally sourced presence, from guardedness to open-hearted participation. Every point along this spectrum offers insight into a unique and necessary phase of group life. No place is better or worse; each carries its own wisdom and emerges to meet a particular need or moment in time.

All points along the Continuum naturally open toward the next. A Conventional group begins to shift as it assumes qualities of the Transitional group. A Transitional group leans toward the New Wave group as it grows more inclusive, aware, and attuned. The New Wave group is not a fixed destination, either. It's a living ideal—always unfolding, always becoming, always expanding the Continuum.

Just as the needs of individuals, communities, and the planet evolve, so do our groups. When we bring awareness to where a group is now, we can sense whether that form is still serving, or if something new is ready to emerge. Whether we're describing a group's habitual experience or noticing what's showing up in a particular moment, every expression is valid. Some gatherings are structured and efficient, while some feel messy but alive. And others become more than the sum of their parts, where everyone feels part of something moving, whole, and wise.

We no longer need to fix or manage a group; we only need to see it more clearly. The key is not to judge but to notice and respond with awareness to new possibilities. If you long for more—more ease, more realness, and more connection and shared intelligence—you don't have to wait for everyone to get on board. Simply how you show up and the attention you bring to what's unfolding can invite a shift and reveal a new way forward.

The Three Groups Continuum is one part of the New Wave of Groups model. In the pages ahead, we'll explore it more deeply, as a way of sensing how each of your groups thinks, acts, and moves. Then we'll turn to the Eight Elements, which offer practical ways to meet any moment right where it is, and make choices that move your groups toward the shifts many long for: more satisfying connection, honest participation, and a sense of real collaboration.

Conventional Groups and Moments– Structure, Clarity, and Safety

For many of us, this is the type of group we've known the longest. Conventional groups are shaped by familiar structures, defined roles, clear expectations, and designated leadership. There's usually a strong sense of who holds the authority and what the group is aiming to achieve. These frameworks offer reliability, order, and a sense of safety.

In many situations, a Conventional group is exactly what supports the moment, especially when stability, specificity, or containment are needed.

What it feels like:
- You know what's expected, and there's comfort in that.

- You may hold back a part of yourself to remain aligned with the group's norms.

- The leader holds responsibility, and others look to them for direction.

- Vulnerability might feel risky or out of place. The heart opens selectively when it feels "safe."

- The group gets things done. Logical thinking prevails; emotional presence or innovation may feel secondary.

Where this shows up:
- A manager sets the agenda, and others take their cues from them.

- A parent says, "Because I said so," and the family knows to follow the plan.

- An educational setting focuses exclusively on the opinions and expertise of the teacher.

- A therapeutic session focuses on guidance or diagnosis rather than co-exploration.

- An inner voice says, "Stick to what you know. Don't mess this up."

When it serves though, this is changing:
- When clarity and efficiency are needed

- In early stages of education or group development

- When structure provides safety or coherence

More and more frequently, groups in this form begin to feel rigid or limiting. It's not a flaw, however. It's often a sign that something new is beginning to move—an invitation to see whether a different way of being together is becoming possible.

Transitional Groups and Moments— Opening, Questioning, and Becoming

Transitional groups are not a static category—they exist on a dynamic continuum. On one end, what we call early Transitional groups still carry many characteristics of Conventional structures, such as reliance on external authority, unspoken norms, and limited individual expression. On the other end, mature Transitional groups are edging toward the qualities of New Wave groups: more fluid roles, deeper authenticity, growing trust in the group field, and a glimpse of unified flow. This movement along the Transitional continuum reflects the group's increasing capacity to sense, trust, and act from a deeper level of collective awareness.

The Transitional group stage is vital. It's where growth happens when we notice what is present, sense what is needed or longed for, and respond with heart. These groups can feel dynamic, messy, even contradictory, but that's exactly what makes them fertile ground for transformation. They hold both the stability of what's known and the invitation of what's possible.

What it feels like:
- You notice the desire to speak more honestly, even if you're unsure how it will land.

- The leader is still present but begins asking questions and inviting input.

- There's a growing awareness of emotional energy in the room.

- Things don't always go smoothly, but something real is happening.

Where this shows up:
- A parent asks their child, "What do you think we should do?" and listens fully.

- A friend group speaks openly about tension, instead of ignoring it.

- A team experiments with decision-making as a shared process.

- An inner dialogue includes both the critic and the wise voice that says, "Let's try a different way."

When it serves:
- When something deeper is longed for

- In creative, healing, or learning environments where voice and presence matter

- When the group is ready to become more alive, co-created, and flexible

New Wave Groups and Moments– Emergence, Coherence, and Unity

In a New Wave group experience, there's a felt sense of unity; not just agreement or connection, but the experience of being part of a living field. Leadership arises organically. Each voice contributes naturally. Silence is welcome. The group moves as one body, guided by something larger than any individual.

When individuals engage in personal development within this field of awareness, they enhance the intelligence of the group itself. Simultaneously, as the group's intelligence expands, individuals can more fully recognize and express their unique gifts and essence. This isn't just a reciprocal process; it's simultaneous and holographic, where the individuals and the group form a unified field of consciousness.

The experience of unity can arise any time we meet each other and the moment with presence, openness, and trust. It has space to emerge when we slow down, listen fully, and release the need to manage expectations or control the outcome.

A New Wave group is not a fixed state; it's an ever-expanding field of awareness. Its unity deepens, its intelligence refines, and its creativity becomes purer, fluid, and more responsive as it evolves.

What it feels like:
- The group feels like its own being—alive, intelligent, and whole. Each person contributes, but no one controls. Instead, there is a sense of something deeper guiding the way.

- You're fully yourself, and fully part of something greater.

- Hearts are open.

- The ego, a self-preservation mechanism, is fully set aside in favor of authentic expression and group attunement.

- Everything belongs and is okay: All emotions, pauses, insights, confusion are valid.

- There's no rush. No fixing. Just presence and trust.

- Insight or healing emerges, without anyone needing to lead.

Where this shows up:
- Two people speak from the heart and drop into shared stillness.

- A creative team moves, as if guided by the same breath.

- A circle attunes to silence and lets something arise from it.

- Inside, your inner parts settle, and there's peace without needing a solution.

- Action arises spontaneously, complete without judgment or evaluation.

When it serves:
A New Wave group or moment is an arising of higher intelligence and deep connection. It is most evident ...

- in spiritual, artistic, or visionary spaces

- during moments of deep trust, vulnerability, or inspiration

- anytime we release the need to manage or shape events or people into what we think they should be, and instead meet what's there, just as it is, with wholehearted presence

The Three Types of Groups

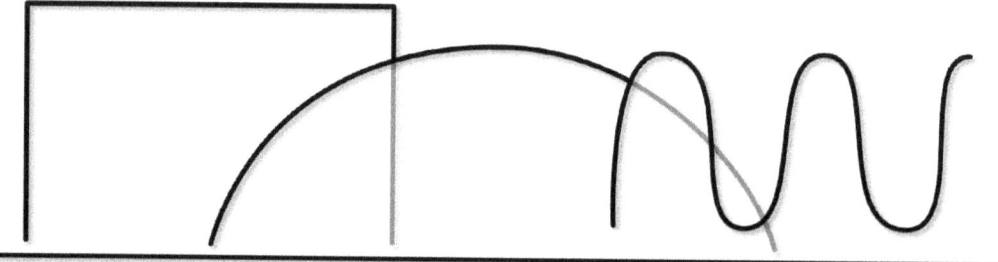

Conventional	Transitional	New Wave
Members identify solely as separate individuals	Members begin to expand self-identification to other and beyond	Members identify both as individuals and group
Ego-centric	Begin acting for common good rather than for personal needs and safety	Ego set aside for the greater good
Open-heartedness contingent upon safety and appropriateness	Hearts opening regardless of circumstance	Hearts open

The Three Types of Groups

Scenario 1: Conflict in a Planning Meeting

Conventional Group:

Two participants begin to disagree about how the project should be structured. One raises their voice. The facilitator interrupts, "Let's move on. We'll take this offline." The group continues, but the energy feels tight. People glance at the clock. The conflict is contained but not addressed. Roles remain fixed; the leader leads, others follow.

Transitional Group:

The disagreement begins. Another participant says, "Can we just hear both ideas fully before choosing?" The group tries to listen, but some people disengage. The facilitator encourages dialogue but subtly favors one side. There's an attempt at openness, yet underneath old dynamics still shape who is heard.

New Wave Group:

The conflict arises. A moment of silence follows. Someone says, "It feels like something deeper is underneath this disagreement. Can we pause and listen to what's really being expressed here?" One person shares vulnerability; another softens. The group leans in. The disagreement becomes a doorway, not a disruption.

Key Insight: Understanding how each group meets the same tension differently—through control, partial openness, or embodied presence—helps readers locate where their group currently lives and what is possible with more awareness.

Scenario 2: Silence After Someone Shares Something Vulnerable

Conventional Group:

A participant shares a personal story about burnout. The room falls silent. The leader quickly says, "Thanks for sharing. Let's turn to the agenda now." The group politely moves on, avoiding discomfort. The silence is filled with productive work.

Transitional Group:

The person shares. The silence feels a bit awkward, but someone says, "Wow, thank you for naming that." Another adds a related story. The group responds with care, but there's still a subtle push to "get back on track." Silence is respected but not yet trusted.

New Wave Group:

The person shares. The group pauses. No one rushes to speak. The silence deepens. The field feels tender, alive. Eventually someone says, "That touched something in me I didn't even know was there." The silence holds presence, not absence. No one is trying to fix anything or anyone. Everyone is with themselves, each other, and the group as a whole.

Key Insight: A group's relationship to silence reveals its level of awareness and trust. In New Wave groups, silence becomes a container for presence and healing, not an interruption to be managed.

Scenario 3: A New Member Joins the Group

Conventional Group:

The new person is welcomed with a few polite words. The leader says, "We usually begin with intros, so please tell us your name and why you're here." The new person speaks briefly. The meeting continues as usual. Roles and procedures are prioritized.

Transitional Group:

The group members take time to introduce themselves. The facilitator asks, "Is there anything you need to feel more at ease here?" There's connection and warmth as the participants follow the agenda. The new person feels included, although not fully part of the group.

New Wave Group:

The group tunes into the field as the new person arrives. Someone says, "Let's take a moment to feel what's shifting as this person joins us." In addition to their names, everyone shares what's alive for them today. The new person is not simply introduced; they are welcomed as part of the resonant connection of the group body.

Key Insight: How a group receives a new member reflects its coherence and awareness. New Wave groups treat relationships as a living field, allowing the group to re-form dynamically with each change.

Observing the Continuum

What matters most is remembering that we are always in motion. Groups fluidly shift across this Continuum. One moment may feel rigid and structured, while another open and emergent. The group qualities are shifting back and forth but continually evolving.

By understanding this continuum—from ego-centric structure to unitive awareness—we develop the ability to notice, sense, and respond more consciously. We stop trying to manage our groups and start listening to them. We stop seeking perfection and begin attuning to presence.

This Three Groups Continuum isn't a path of improvement—it's a way of noticing. Each group state has value and contributes something essential. The opportunity is to notice where we are and recognize what it may be serving now, and what it may be opening toward next.

There's no pressure to push a group forward. Sometimes, the predictability of a Conventional group is what's needed. Sometimes, a Transitional group is the perfect place to grow and stretch. And sometimes a New Wave moment arrives. Not because we chase it, but because we're ready to let it move through us.

This is the gift of awareness: noticing where we are, sensing what's needed, and meeting the moment with presence and care.

Cultural Lenses on Leadership and Participation

This book is written from an individualist, Western cultural perspective (common in North America, much of Europe, and Australia). In contrast, many collectivist cultures—found across much of East Asia, Southeast Asia, Africa, the Middle East, and Latin America, and among many indigenous peoples—emphasize very different ways of understanding leadership and participation.

In collectivist cultures, leadership is often about maintaining harmony and serving the whole rather than asserting an individual vision. Leaders may be respected as stewards of group well-being, guiding more through presence, subtle influence, or shared values than through personal authority. Participation also leans toward contribution to the group rather than individual self-expression. Decisions are often made by consensus, and members may refrain from bringing forward something that could disrupt unity.

These qualities resonate with the heart of the New Wave perspective: The recognition that we are arising as the being of the group, not just as separate individuals. Collectivist orientations can strengthen the movement toward coherence and shared awareness.

At the same time, when harmony is highly valued, a different balance of expression emerges. Transparency and emergence may be tempered in order to protect relationship and unity. This does not mean people are withholding what is "real," but that what is considered authentic is expressed in a way that prioritizes collective well-being. In some contexts, this can keep a group in more of a Transitional tone, while still carrying deep integrity.

In more individualist cultures, the opposite challenge appears. People may feel freer to express themselves openly, but the group can fragment into competing agendas and identities, adhering more to the Conventional structure. Here, the task is learning to soften self-assertion into a unitive perspective honoring the whole.

If your context is collectivist, some of the practices here may already feel natural, while others may invite you to experiment with more direct transparency or individual expression than is customary. You may find resonance in unexpected places or choose to adapt the elements to your own cultural rhythms. What matters isn't adopting a "Western" model, but sensing how the principles of coherence, authenticity, and group awareness are already alive in your setting, and how they might deepen.

Evolutionary groups ask us to bring forward both gifts: the collectivist heartfelt attunement to the whole and the individualist courage to voice one's truth. Unity consciousness emerges not from suppressing differences or from overemphasizing autonomy, but from recognizing that authenticity shows up differently across cultures and that the group field comes alive when each form of authentic expression is welcomed as an equally valuable part of the whole.

This is where the Eight Elements come in. Welcome to the journey.

PART III

The Eight Elements That Move Any Group Toward Unity Consciousness

To be more is to be more united.
— Pierre Teilhard de Chardin, The Human Phenomenon

Introduction to the Eight Elements

The Eight Elements are the heart of our guidebook—essential shifts in attention and orientation that can change how a group feels, functions, and evolves. Each element invites a deeper level of presence, receptivity, and awareness of the group as a living being.

Instead of serving as tools to fix a group, the elements are gentle invitations to meet any moment with more spaciousness and heart. They are ways for you, as an individual, to sense the group field and select qualities you'd like to bring forward right now. They help reveal what is naturally emerging: greater wholeness, deeper connection, and more authentic creativity. You can turn toward the Eight Elements in an instant or return to them over time. Together, they offer a practical, intuitive path for participating in any group with more awareness and aliveness.

You've explored the landscape of Conventional, Transitional, and New Wave groups. Now it's time for you to explore the Eight Elements—qualities of presence that can actively guide any group toward self-awareness, coherence, and unity consciousness. Even a single moment of leaning into one can shift the intelligence and tone of the entire group field, whether you are a gathering of two or twenty.

While we have numbered the elements for ease of reference, they are not a sequence to follow. Each one is always present and interwoven with the others. You might commit to one element as a guiding practice for a while, or you might glance at the list and feel inexplicably drawn to one in that particular moment. Often, there's more at play than deciding what you think will help—it's closer to attuning to what's quietly calling you.

Committing to all Eight Elements generates a potent, living field—one alive and responsive in ways that support coherence, emergence, and transformation, regardless of the content you bring into it. You can place anything into this field—a meeting, a conversation, a conflict, a challenge—and its evolution, and any needed "healing," will accelerate. This isn't an imposed structure; it is a spacious invitation for a higher order of intelligence to unfold. In such a field, things move

31

with greater ease, and there is a shared awareness that what is emerging is fresh, alive, and full of promise.

You don't need to begin in any particular place. Start anywhere: with the opening of a chapter, a story, a prompt, or a practice. Let the element you are drawn to meet you right where you are and allow it to shape what comes next.

Let the journey surprise you. We wish you joy and fascination as it unfolds.

Element One

Attending to the Presence of Silence

Silence is essential. We need silence just as much as we need
air, just as much as plants need light. If our minds are crowded
with words and thoughts, there is no space for us.
—*Thich Nhat Hanh*

Silence is one of the great arts of conversation.
—*Cicero*

You may read this chapter on its own, or as part of the full sequence of the Eight Elements That Move Any Group Toward Unity Consciousness. Explore all eight if that is what interests you in the moment or simply pause with the one that calls you. Each element is a passageway to the new quality of group experience.

This element invites us to notice and embrace the moments of quiet that naturally arise within group interactions.

Silence is not something to rush past or fill. It is a potent space of stillness and rest, where integration, clarity, potential, and deeper connection can arise. In silence, we have the chance to listen more fully, both to ourselves and to others.

By intentionally acknowledging and allowing space for silence, groups create an environment from which deeper wisdom, genuine understanding, and authentic insights can emerge.

How Silence Is Experienced in the Three Groups

In the Three Groups model, we recognize that the relationship to silence manifests differently, depending on where the group is along its evolutionary continuum.

Conventional Groups

Conventional groups often experience silence as uncomfortable, awkward, or empty. Silence may—even must—be quickly filled with words, tasks, or authority-driven redirection to maintain control, structure, and the comfort of familiarity.

Transitional Groups

Transitional groups begin to tolerate and even value silence, seeing it as a space for reflection or a necessary pause. However, they may still view it as an interruption to "productive" interaction rather than a vital presence.

New Wave Groups

New Wave groups embrace silence as an alive presence in itself. It's not merely an absence of speaking, but a potent field that can stand on its own. Silence becomes a co-participant, holding the potential for connection and attunement.

Element One: Attending to the Presence of Silence

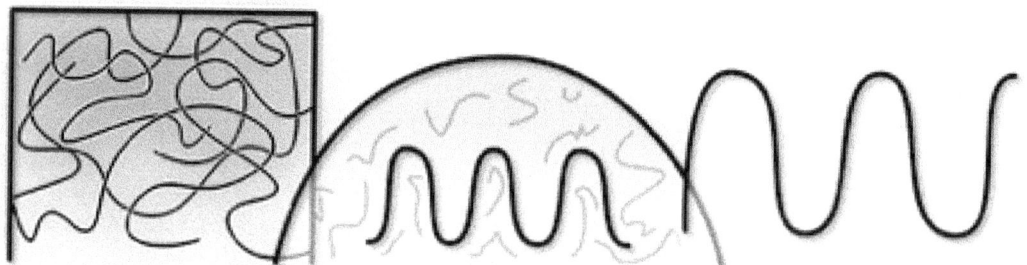

Conventional

Rarely any silence, and then uncomfortable

Considered a deficiency or a vacuum

Customarily must be filled

Transitional

Practicing listening for, recognizing, and making room for silence

Acknowledged as its own presence

Recognition that creative or higher intelligence often needs silence to be known

New Wave

Silence has equal presence in the unity

Fully attended to by all participants

Living the Element

You've explored the essence of this element; now comes the invitation to practice it. The sections that follow suggest when it may be most helpful, how it can take shape, and ways to deepen it with those around you.

When to Use
- Practice Attending to Silence regularly, particularly when clarity, understanding, or deeper connection is desired.

- Silence is especially valuable when group interactions feel rushed, reactive, disconnected, or confused.

- Embrace silence intentionally, whenever the atmosphere feels noisy, unsettled, or fragmented.

- Silence is particularly valuable when someone does not feel heard or included, or feels misunderstood.

How to Use
- Silence often tries to make itself felt—we've simply learned to override our natural awareness of it.

- Begin to notice and tune in to the subtle cues you may feel in your body or in the atmosphere of the group. Practice noticing and following the cues. Simply stop and allow silence, even if it feels risky.

- Let go of any expectations about what should happen, how long it should last, or how it should feel. Simply let the silence be what it is right now.

- Practice tolerating the silence for longer periods, sitting within it, surrendering to it. Nothing to do. Just stop, rest. Be quiet in your body and, if possible, in your mind.

- Simply be within the silence, until the next spontaneous arising occurs.

- Treat silence like another "voice at the table." Give it time for expression before naturally moving on.

What You Might Say

- I would just like a moment of silence.

- I need a moment of silence.

- Let's take a breath, sit for a moment, and then see where we are.

- I've been noticing how powerful it can be when we don't rush to fill every pause. Sometimes, a little silence actually deepens the conversation—or lets something more real happen.

- Attending to silence means noticing when it arises and allowing it to be, without rushing to fill it with words or actions. Silence creates space to listen more deeply, to take in what has been said, to sense our own responses, and to move forward from connection rather than from habit.

Exercises and Practical Applications

For Families

Brief Silent Moments
Regularly take brief pauses (a couple of breaths or 20 seconds) during conversations or meals, allowing family members to rest and notice themselves quietly.

Family Silence Activity
Designate quiet family activities, such as short silent walks or sitting quietly together in nature. Afterward, gently share reflections or insights experienced during the silence.

Prompts to Explore Together
Parents
- I feel most connected to my family when we quietly _____.

- Silence feels most comfortable at home when _____.

- When I allow silence during difficult family conversations, I notice _____.

- One way our family could benefit from more silence is _____.

- A moment when silence deeply helped our family was _____.

Children
- Silence helps me feel calmer when I _____.

- When my family sits silently together, I feel _____.

- One thing I notice when I'm quiet is _____.

- I would like more silent time at home because _____.

- Silence makes me feel closer to my family when _____.

For Businesses

Silent Integration
Introduce brief periods of silence after significant ideas are shared during meetings, allowing everyone to integrate what was expressed.

Reflective Silence Sessions
Schedule dedicated sessions where complex challenges are first addressed through silent reflection. Then allow participants to share insights that naturally emerged.

Prompts to Explore Together
- Our team's most insightful ideas emerge when we silently _____.

- Silence during meetings helps me _____.

- I find silence challenging at work because _____.

- Our workplace could benefit from regular silence by _____.

- One significant insight I gained during a silent pause was _____.

- When silence arises naturally, I feel _____.

- I tend to fill silence because _____, but I'd like to try_____.

- The potential benefit of silence at work that excites me is _____.

- When our team integrates silence, we tend to _____.

- Silence helps our team become more effective by _____.

For Social Groups

Moment of Quiet Alignment
Begin social gatherings with brief silence (1–2 minutes), inviting everyone to become present, grounded, and energetically connected.

Shared Silent Experiences
Organize silent activities like meditation, silent meals, campfire gazing, or nature walks, and then afterward gently explore the insights that emerged.

Prompts to Explore Together
- When our social group includes silence, I notice _____.

- Silence feels most natural with friends when we _____.

- I would appreciate more moments of quiet rest and silence where we could _____.

- Our group becomes more authentic when we allow silence to _____.

- One silent experience I've enjoyed with friends was _____.

- I believe we could incorporate more silence in our gatherings by _____.

- My resistance to silence in social settings comes from _____.

- Silence improves our group interactions by _____.

- The most surprising insight I've had during group silence was _____.

- I would like our group to intentionally practice silence because _____.

- Silence deepens our friendship by _____.

For Support / Therapy Groups

Silent Opening
Begin sessions with brief, intentional silence, allowing participants to settle and reconnect with themselves.

Deeper Silence Exploration
Incorporate longer periods of silence during sessions, encouraging participants to notice what arises internally, followed by sharing.

Leader Practices
Model Comfort with Silence: Regularly integrate brief silences, demonstrating their value and normalizing their presence.

Facilitate Reflective Silence: Create intentional spaces for silence after important contributions to allow deeper integration.

Participant Practices
Inner Listening: Allow yourself moments of silence to turn inward, noticing thoughts, sensations, and insights.

Making Space for Yourself: Ask your therapist to pause if you need some silence to absorb and integrate what they are saying.

Valuing Quiet Spaces: Actively appreciate silence as a resource for self-awareness.

Prompts to Explore Together

- When our group sits silently together, I experience _____.

- Silence helps me connect more deeply with myself by _____.

- One insight that emerged from group silence was _____.

- During silence, I usually feel _____, and I would like to explore why.

- I notice our group feels more cohesive after periods of silence. I think this is because _____.

- Silence can sometimes feel uncomfortable when _____.

- My intention for embracing silence more fully is _____.

- The most comforting thing about silence in this session is _____.

- I am learning to appreciate silence as a valuable tool for _____.

- Silent moments help me appreciate and integrate discussions by _____.

For Individuals (Self-Awareness and Inner Dialogue)

Micro-pause Practice

Set a timer for three random times daily. When it rings, simply stop whatever you're doing and remain still for 30 seconds. No need to do anything. Just notice the quality of silence around and within you. Allow the nervous system to reset and return to the present moment.

Stillness Inquiry

Sit quietly and ask yourself, "What's beneath this thought? And beneath that?" Follow your awareness layer by layer into silence—not as absence, but as a presence that holds it all. Journal afterward on any shift you noticed in tone, sensation, or insight.

Prompts to Explore

- When I let myself become quiet, what I begin to notice is _____.

- A surprising way that silence showed up for me today was _____.

- The difference between quiet outside me and quiet inside me feels like _____.

- When I don't rush to respond, I hear _____.

Navigating Challenges

- Remind group members or clients that silence is natural and valuable. It is something to welcome rather than avoid or hurry through.

- Notice and name the cues that indicate that silence is emerging—such as a sense in the body that a pause would be welcome; a moment of mental confusion that needs time to settle; or a strong emotion that could benefit from a few breaths of space.

- Offer gentle reassurance when discomfort with silence arises.

- Practice letting silence naturally end or continue, as needed.

- When we embrace silence in a group or in our private space, we open a passageway to inner stillness, allowing our nervous system to settle, deeper truths to surface, and a more mature intelligence to guide our next steps.

Scenario

Every evening at dinner, 7-year-old Max chatters nonstop—about school, his gaming world, what the dog did, and what he might do tomorrow. His father, who longs for even a moment of quiet connection, often feels overwhelmed but doesn't want to repress Max's enthusiasm.

One evening, instead of asking Max to be quiet, his dad gently says, "Hey Max, want to try a one-minute experiment with me? Let's both close our eyes and see if we can hear the tiniest sound in the room."

Max pauses, intrigued. For the first time all day, the kitchen fills with silence, followed by the sound of the refrigerator humming, a dog sighing, and the clink of a fork on a plate. Something shifts. When they open their eyes, Max smiles, his voice a little softer he says, "I heard my own breathing."

Element Two

Opening the Heart by Nurturing a Unitive Perspective (No Right, Wrong, or Judgment)

When you go into the woods and look at trees, you see all these different trees. And some of them are bent, and some of them are straight... And you look at the tree and you allow it. You appreciate it. You see why it is the way it is. You sort of understand... But the minute you get near humans, you lose all that. And you are constantly saying 'You're too this,' or 'I'm too this.' That judging mind comes in. So I practice turning people into trees. Which means appreciating them just the way they are.

—*Ram Dass*

This element is about seeing through the eyes of the heart rather than with the judging mind. It invites us to drop our need to sort things into right and wrong, good and bad, useful or not useful categories. Equally important, it invites us to receive everything that arises in a group—every comment, feeling, disagreement, even silence—as an equally valuable part of the unfolding.

This isn't just a lofty idea; it's something real, grounded, and practical. When we loosen the mind's grip on judgment and allow the heart to take its place at the center, new pathways open. Dialogue deepens. Conflict softens. And the group begins to feel more alive, more whole—because it is being held, even briefly, in the spaciousness of unity.

When every contribution is held as valuable, we begin to see each moment as meaningful. All voices and perspectives are simply information about the group, ourselves, and what might be trying to emerge.

When we stop labeling things as problems or mistakes, we begin to recognize the deeper intelligence already at work.

This shift doesn't require perfection. It asks only for a little more space in how we listen—for a little more room in the heart. And the more we practice this way of being, the more the group becomes a place where people feel safe, connected, and able to show up fully.

How Opening the Heart by Nurturing a Unitive Perspective Is Experienced in the Three Groups

Conventional Groups

In Conventional groups, there's usually a strong sense of what's right and wrong. People try to say the "correct" thing. Differences can feel like problems to solve or positions to defend. The heart tends to open only to what feels familiar or safe.

Transitional Groups

In Transitional groups, we start to stretch. We try to hold more perspectives at once and notice when we're judging. We practice tolerating paradox rather than being attached to a side. It can still feel messy or effortful, especially in moments of stress, but there's more awareness and more willingness to stay open.

New Wave Groups

In New Wave groups, something shifts. We begin to trust that everything showing up is part of the whole. Even tension or confusion is viewed as helpful, because it reveals something important. In fact, all expressions and events are useful information. There's freedom in not having to evaluate or fix—just allowing what is. We pay attention with the whole group body, knowing that a deeper truth is emerging.

This way of seeing softens resistance and invites curiosity. When we open our hearts, we step into something larger than our need to take a side or assign value. From there, the unity that we truly are becomes our common experience

Element Two: Opening The Heart By Nurturing A Unitive Perspective

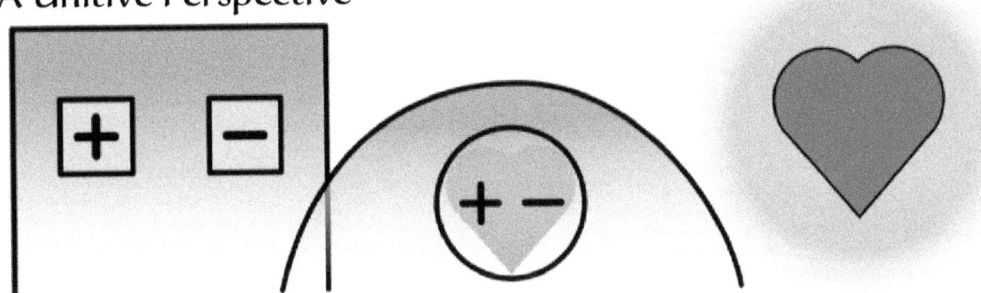

Conventional	Transitional	New Wave
Good or bad	Good and bad	Neutrality
Duality	Paradox	Unity
Right vs. wrong, useful vs. not	Stretching perception to hold all	Experienced as an individual and as the group
Separate, individual	Trying not to judge or prefer	No other, therefore, no comparison
Comparative	Loosening attraction to the "right" position	All fundamentally good (i.e., all just information)
Selectively open heart based upon appraisal of value	Striving to keep heart open	

Living the Element

You've explored the essence of this element; now comes the invitation to practice it. The sections that follow suggest when it may be most helpful, how it can take shape, and ways to deepen it with those around you.

When to Use

Nurturing a Unitive Perspective can shift a room, soften defenses, and open hearts. Here are some moments when turning toward it can make all the difference:

- When there's tension or misunderstanding: Conflict, emotional reactions, or opposing views can easily fragment a group. In these moments, the unitive perspective invites us to pause, soften, and widen the lens. It asks, "What else is here? What might we be missing when we only view from one side?"

- When defensiveness, judgment, or reactivity arise: Rather than reacting from separation, this element helps you return to curiosity and compassion. Even a breath, a glance, or a question asked from the heart can shift the atmosphere.

- When someone is hurting or struggling to express something: The unitive perspective doesn't try to fix. It holds. It listens with the whole self. It allows space for emotion without collapsing into it.

- When things are going well, but you sense the potential for more: This element isn't just for problems. Use it when you want to go deeper, not because something is wrong, but because something more is possible. It invites intimacy, presence, and mutual discovery.

- When you want to see someone more fully: Whether in silence or in conversation, this element invites you to meet others beyond their words or roles—to feel who they are underneath the surface.

- When a moment feels tender or beautiful: The unitive perspective lets you stay with the subtle, sacred quality of connection. It allows you to take in the goodness of being together.

- When the group is fragmented—or flowing: Whether things feel stuck or alive, this element is always available. It's not about changing the situation but about entering it more consciously.

- Anytime you want to meet others in essence, not just in function: This is the heart of unitive awareness—not to solve, perform, or perfect—but to be fully present and remember we are not separate.

What You Might Say

- A unitive perspective helps us see beyond judgments or differences, encouraging connection, compassion, and mutual understanding.

- Opening our hearts to a unitive perspective means consciously setting aside our judgments and fixed ideas about what's right or wrong, good or bad. Instead, we choose curiosity, neutrality, and compassion. When we do so, we create a safe and open space where deeper truth and authentic connections are able to emerge.

Exercises and Practical Applications

For Families

Gratitude Sharing
Hold brief family meetings where each person shares something they genuinely appreciate about another.

Neutral Listening Practice
Practice family conversations where one person speaks openly about their experiences or feelings, while others listen silently without judgment, evaluation, or response. Fully receiving someone's expression can be a powerfully validating event.

Prompts to Explore Together
These prompts encourage curiosity, introspection, compassion, and deeper understanding, and open the group to more inclusion and connection.

Parents
- When my child expresses something that I don't agree with, I usually respond by _____. However, I would like to respond by _____.

- To foster openness, our family conversations will include more _____.

- I want my children to feel safe expressing differences because _____.

- One judgment I can release about my parenting is _____.

- Our family atmosphere becomes kinder when I consciously choose to _____.

Children

- I feel safest sharing my true feelings when my family _____.

- One thing I wish my family understood about me is _____.

- Instead of judging, I could show kindness by _____.

- I appreciate my family more when they _____.

- If I disagree with _____ at home, I'd like to handle it by _____.

For Businesses

Neutral Language Check

Set a group intention to avoid judgmental language during meetings. Gently remind each other when judgments arise, refocusing discussions on facts, curiosity, and openness.

Perspective-Taking Exercise

Periodically invite team members to articulate a colleague's viewpoint on important issues. This validates empathy, reduces misunderstanding, and enhances inclusion.

Prompts to Explore Together

- I find it easier to suspend judgment of my colleagues when I _____.

- Our team atmosphere improves significantly when we focus on _____.

- One specific judgment our team could collectively release is _____.

- Instead of seeing differing opinions as prolems, we could view them as _____.

- Neutrality at work helps me personally to _____.

- I could contribute to a more accepting workplace culture by _____.

- When a conflict arises, our team's immediate step might be _____.

- Judgment-free communication at work allows me to _____.

- I'd like to remind our team regularly that our shared intention is _____.

For Social Groups

No-Judgment Circle
Begin social gatherings with each person briefly sharing something meaningful without any feedback or critique. Simply acknowledge and appreciate each contribution.

Empathy Role-Playing
Playfully conduct role-playing scenarios that invite members to take on perspectives very different from their own, helping to dissolve judgments and foster deeper understanding.

Prompts to Explore Together
- Our friendships deepen when we let go of judgments about _____.

- I can contribute to more compassionate conversations by _____.

- Our group's energy improves dramatically when we focus on _____.

- An assumption I'm willing to release about others in our group is _____.

- The feeling I'd like to cultivate more in our group is _____.

- I really love everyone in the group. My judgments cause me to _____.

- To reduce judgments, our group could regularly practice _____.

- The unspoken judgment I carry that I'd like to release is _____.

- To foster unity, I will intentionally practice _____.

- Our shared group intention for openness and neutrality is _____.

For Support / Therapy Groups

Compassionate Mirroring

Pair members for brief sharing, with each listener reflecting back the speaker's words without judgment, interpretation, or advice.

Judgment Journaling

Invite each participant to maintain a private journal where they record judgments noticed during group interactions. Periodically, invite neutral sharing of insights from these journals to support collective growth and self-awareness.

Leader Practices

Model Neutrality: Consistently demonstrate openness, neutrality, and compassion, especially during challenging interactions.

Neutral Facilitation: Guide discussions with gentle reminders to remain curious and compassionate, especially when tensions arise.

Prompts to Explore Together

- When I feel judged, I typically respond by _____. Instead, I'd prefer to _____.

- My healing deepens when I accept _____ without judgment.

- The judgment I'm ready to let go of about myself is _____.

- Our group feels most supportive when we remember to _____.

- A perspective I'd like our group to hold more consistently is _____.

Participant Practices

Internal Reflection: Regularly notice when personal judgments arise and consciously choose to approach them with curiosity and compassion rather than reaction.

Neutral Listening: Practice listening to others without immediate reaction, judgment, or evaluation. Note if this shifts what you notice about them or how you feel.

Prompts to Explore Together
- I feel compassion in the group most strongly when _____.

- Judgments in our group are reduced significantly when we _____.

- My openness increases greatly when I notice _____.

- One way I can practice neutrality in group discussions is by _____.

- I feel most connected to the group when there is an absence of _____.

For Individuals (Self-Awareness and Inner Dialogue)

Heart-Centered Reframe
When you judge or label yourself, pause and ask, "What might be another way to see this?" Shift into curiosity and compassion rather than self-blame.

Inner Voices Dialogue
Write a dialogue between two contrasting inner voices—one critical, one tender. Let them speak honestly to each other. Then, invite a third voice to enter: one that holds both, with neutrality and love. Explore how all parts are seeking wholeness.

Prompts to Explore
- A judgment I noticed today (toward myself or another) was _____.

- When I soften my stance and listen more attentively, I begin to see _____.

- A place where I'm holding tight to "being right" is _____.

- What if both parts of this conflict have something true to say?

Navigating Challenges

Gently and openly address judgments or misunderstandings when they surface, reaffirming the group's commitment to neutrality and compassion.

Recognize that cultivating a unitive perspective is an ongoing practice requiring patience, continuous effort, and mutual support.

By nurturing a unitive perspective, groups expand their capacity for genuine connection, deeper insight, and harmonious interactions—significantly enriching their shared experiences and moving toward greater unity consciousness.

Scenario

In a family discussion, a member says something controversial. Another member snaps, "That's not how it works." Tension rises.

The parent could intervene, but instead says, "Can we pause? I want to try something. Can each of us, just for a moment, consider that what's true for one person doesn't cancel out what's true for another?"

A silence opens. Then someone says, "I got scared. I didn't mean to shut you down. I'm sorry."

The first person softens. "Thanks. I know I burst in angrily sometimes, too."

Key Insight: When a group releases the need to label right/wrong and instead nurtures an open-hearted, unitive perspective, members feel safer to stay present even in difference. This element makes room for truth to emerge in a way that builds connection instead of fracture.

Element Three

Awareness and Acknowledgment of Higher Intelligence

In the beginning is the relation. When we meet each other in authenticity, a real presence is born—not just between us, but as us.
—*Martin Buber*

A 2023 Pew Research Center study shows that over 90 percent of the world's population believes in some form of higher intelligence. Whether called Nature, God, Ancestors, Source, Spirit, the Universe, Beauty, one's Higher Self, or something else entirely, these beliefs span cultures, languages, and traditions, reflecting a deep human intuition that something greater is present, informing and perhaps guiding life.

This element invites you to turn toward one particular expression of higher intelligence: the living presence that emerges when people gather. We suggest that something real and responsive comes alive through the group itself—an intelligence that can be sensed, received, and moved with. It arises not from outside us, but through our shared presence, arising only when people gather. It is more than the sum of its parts, and often more than we realize in the moment.

This element isn't tied to any religion or spiritual path but leaves space for all types of religious and spiritual practices and traditions. It's useful to anyone because it points to something we all have access to: the deeper presence that often becomes noticeable when people come together with sincerity and attention.

Insights from neuroscience, collective intelligence, intersubjective practice, and group dialogue are beginning to support what ancient traditions and lived experience have long suggested: Intelligence is not confined to individuals. Something wiser emerges when we gather with honesty, presence, and an open orientation.

53

As we attune to it, groups often discover insights, solutions, and creativity that reach far beyond what any single person alone could generate.

This possibility is often overlooked, as most of us have not been taught that it exists or how to benefit from it. In groups, our attention typically stays on tasks, personalities, or outcomes. We seldom pause to notice what's moving through the group as a whole. But when we do, something profound shifts.

Sensing this deeper presence doesn't require special training—only a willingness to slow down, to be present, and to consider that what moves through a group may be more than the sum of its parts. What each of us is expressing is arising from another, higher order of intelligence.

How to Begin

Sensing Higher Intelligence in Practice

Begin by turning your attention gently inward and outward at the same time. Let your awareness stretch beyond your individual identity—beyond your roles, plans, or need to know—and open to the sense that something more might be present. You do not need to do or know anything more.

This is not about belief. It's a simple, quiet shift. A loosening of control. A willingness to let go of your grip on how things should unfold, and just to be, relaxing into the possibility of something larger at work.

Often, just one person making this simultaneous inward/outward orientation changes the tone. A pause. A breath. A moment of naming the possibility that something deeper may be available. When this happens—when even a few in the group orient toward higher intelligence, without letting go of their self-identity—the space opens. The group attends in a different way.

Insight might arise from an unexpected place. Someone may speak from a deeper layer. The whole purpose of the gathering might subtly shift, and what emerges isn't forced. It feels inspired, timely, or quietly right.

This practice begins with attention. It unfolds with trust. And it doesn't require effort—only presence.

The "Being of the Group"

Naming the Presence That Arises as Us

What if the "something greater" isn't far away or abstract—but right here, woven into the space through, between, and within us?

In the New Wave groups, we call this the "being of the group." It's a way of naming the real, felt presence that can arise when people come together with sincerity and attention. This presence is not just a mood or a metaphor. It's a lived quality of awareness that emerges from the group itself, as the group itself—not from any one person, but how we all perceive when being together.

You may have sensed it before, in a moment of silence after someone speaks truthfully, or in the way a room seems to breathe differently when a group suddenly lands on a shared understanding. It's subtle but unmistakable. In moments like these, the being of the group is more clearly felt.

You don't need to believe in anything mystical to sense it. Just consider that when we gather, there may be more available than we typically notice—not just a larger number of ideas, but more intelligence. More presence. More connection. More possibility. Turning toward that presence, even quietly and inwardly, helps it become more perceptible. Naming it together, even simply, makes it more available.

And when we include it in how we listen, speak, and move, the group doesn't just function better—it begins to become aware. What emerges is more than col-laboration. The group moves toward being a unified field of awareness: a shared living presence that can sense, respond, and create in ways no individual alone could generate. In this state, something new becomes possible, not because anyone is trying harder, but because the group is cohering at a deeper level. The field itself is aware.

(For a fuller experience of what we call a Self-Aware Group—a New Wave group that recognizes itself as a living being—see the appendix: Qualities of a Self-Aware New Wave Group.)

How Awareness and Acknowledgment of Higher Intelligence is Experienced in the Three Groups

Conventional Groups

If any awareness of higher intelligence is present in the group, it's not usually acknowledged. If it's acknowledged, the person generally considers themselves to be assisted by higher intelligence, not partnered with it. Language referring to intelligence beyond our own may feel uncomfortable or inappropriate, except in a religious or spiritual setting.

Transitional Groups

There is acknowledgment of higher intelligence in many forms e.g., higher self, being of the group, Earth, spiritual figures, star beings, God, The Universe, Great Spirit, etc. Speaking awareness out loud is more frequent. Groups and individuals begin to turn toward higher intelligence more regularly. There may be a developing awareness of partnership, but higher intelligence is still often seen as an "outside" authority.

New Wave Groups

"We are part of the higher intelligence!"

Element Three: Awareness and Acknowledgment of Higher Intelligence

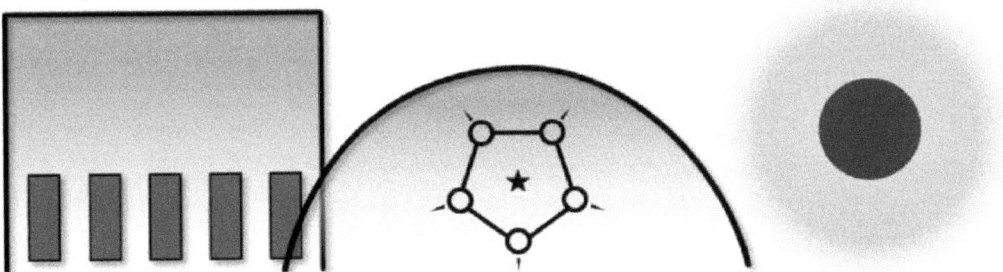

Conventional

If any awareness of higher intelligence, not usually acknowledged

Not spoken unless in the culture (e.g., religious group)

If acknowledged, higher intelligence is considered to be "other than" or "outside of" the individual

Transitional

Acknowledgment of higher intelligence in many forms (e.g., higher self, being of the group, Earth, Beauty, spiritual figures, star beings, God, The Universe, Great Spirit, etc.)

Speaking awareness out loud is more frequent

Developing habit to turn toward higher intelligence

Possible awareness of partnership but still often higher intelligence as an outside authority

New Wave

"We are a part of higher intelligence."

Living the Element

You've explored the essence of this element; now comes the invitation to practice it. The sections that follow suggest when it may be most helpful, how it can take shape, and ways to deepen it with those around you.

When to Use

Awareness and Acknowledgment of Higher Intelligence is always relevant and useful. It can be particularly powerful:

- At the start of a gathering, to center the group in something larger than individual agendas

- In moments of confusion or disagreement, when clarity seems out of reach

- When the group feels fragmented, flat, or overly mental, and you sense that something deeper can surface

- In celebration or gratitude, to recognize the invisible intelligence that made a moment of grace possible

- When someone shares something vulnerable or true, and you want to attune to what's now alive in the group field

- When you're stuck in self-focus—worrying about how you're being perceived or what to say next—and you long to reconnect to presence

- In creative processes, where new ideas or pathways are needed and the usual approaches feel limited

- In times of quiet joy, to deepen the group's connection to what is already flowing well

- When you're about to make a decision and want to open to a broader perspective

- When you feel the group, or yourself, straining, pushing, or trying too hard, and there's a need to soften and allow

More than a technique, this is a shift in posture. It's a turning of attention—not the action to solve or figure out but to rest in the awareness of a larger field, the being that is already present and available. When we turn toward higher intelligence, we often enter a space where certainty dissolves and the mind recedes. We find ourselves in the mystery—not looking for answers but surrendering to something greater than our individuality. For this one moment, we have let go of our ego, and with that, the need to control, to know, or to be right.

What You Might Say

- I appreciate the quality of heart and intelligence that is always here when we gather.

- I'm taking a moment to relax and turn my attention to the larger intelligence that is present because the two of us are meeting.

- Sometimes, I get the sense that there's something bigger holding the group—like a deeper intelligence we can listen to together. It's not about any one person having the answer, but about tuning into something more whole.

- Awareness and Acknowledgment of Higher Intelligence invites us to consciously tune into the collective wisdom emerging from our interconnected presence. It involves trusting that when we genuinely connect and listen, powerful insights and creativity naturally arise, guiding us toward aligned inspired action.

Exercises and Practical Applications

In any group, try this: Pause for just a moment. Soften your focus. Sense the whole. You may begin to notice a presence that isn't coming from any one person, but from the group of all of you.

In meditation and/or throughout the day, come to a place of quiet observation and sense the "group body" of any group in which you find yourself. Notice its personality. Consider the state of its energy (Calm? Frenetic?). Can you sense a purpose to the gathering? What quality of participation and/or leadership does it elicit from you?

Added Focus

Imagine if everyone in your group were to set aside their primary identification with the individual ego and allow themselves to gently "rest into" a conscious awareness of the entire group. Name at least five ways this orientation / focus of awareness affects you (e.g., How do you personally feel now that you are resting as the group being? How do you feel toward the others? Does your role or position in the group change? How do you show up? Where is the authority of the group? What impulses do you notice? From where does "information" arise?)

For Families

Family Wisdom Circle

Take a few quiet minutes together as a family to pause and settle. You might close your eyes, take a few breaths, or just sit quietly. You can say something like, "Let's turn toward the wisdom we are together as a group."

Then, when someone feels ready, they can share a thought, feeling, or quiet knowing about a question or situation they as an individual, or you all as a group, are sitting with. There's no need to explain or respond—just let each voice be heard and held.

Each person's sharing is welcomed without discussion or debate—just received with appreciation.

Intuition Journal

Each family member maintains a journal to capture intuitive insights or dreams that arise, sharing meaningful insights periodically during family gatherings.

Prompts to Explore Together

- When I soften and simply sit with our family, what I begin to sense is _____.

- As I turn toward the being of our family—not our roles, but our shared presence, I notice _____.

- A quality I feel when I stop trying to fix or manage anything in this family is _____.

- If I let go of what I think should happen, what quietly arises in me is _____.

- When I imagine our family as one being, what I sense is _____.

- A moment I felt the intelligence of the whole family moving was _____.

- When I'm simply present with everyone here, what I feel most is _____.

- The spaciousness around us right now feels like _____.

- What begins to come alive when we are just together, without needing to do anything, is _____.

For Businesses

Collective Insight Check-In
Begin meetings with a short silence, inviting team members to briefly share any intuitive insights about the agenda or challenges at hand. (Each speak for maybe 2 minutes, without going into conversation.)

Wisdom Integration Session
Hold dedicated sessions for exploring complex issues solely through intuitive inquiry. Participants may share spontaneous insights, noticing themes or patterns without immediate analysis, allowing the group's higher intelligence to guide next steps.

Prompts to Explore Together
- When I shift from thinking individually to sensing the team as a whole, what I notice is _____.

- If something deeper is moving through our work together, it might feel like _____.

- As I pause and feel into the field of this team, what I begin to sense is _____.

- When we stop pushing and just let the group breathe, what arises is _____.

- The quality I sense in our shared attention right now is _____.

- If this team were one being, its presence would feel like _____.

- I sense we're most aligned as a group when _____.

- Something subtle and intelligent that seems to be forming in this group is _____.

- When I turn toward what we're becoming, not just what we're doing, I feel _____.

For Social Groups

Intuition-Sharing Round
Begin gatherings by inviting each person to briefly share an intuitive insight or feeling that they've experienced recently, fostering a deeper group connection.

Group Wisdom Visualization
Guide the group through a spacious visualization exercise where everyone imagines connecting to the group's collective wisdom, then openly sharing what emerges.

Prompts to Explore Together
- When I sit with this group without needing to speak, what begins to stir in me is _____.

- If our connection had a tone or a presence, it would feel like _____.

- As I turn toward our shared space, not just the people in it, I sense _____.

- A quality I feel when we are simply being together, without effort, is _____.

- When I pause and feel the "us" of this group, I notice _____.

- I sense that something subtle becomes possible in us when _____.

- If this group had a deeper voice or feeling today, it might be _____.

- When I soften into presence here, what emerges is _____.

- The spaciousness I feel around and within this group is _____.

- Being with this group field today, I'm aware of _____.

For Support / Therapy Groups

Leader Practices

Attuning to the Group Field: Begin each session by inviting everyone to pause for a few breaths together. Rather than going right into personal sharing, ask each person to sense into the larger presence of the group itself—the atmosphere, tone, or "heart" that is here when you gather. After a short silence, participants can offer a word, gesture, or image that reflects what they sense in the group field. This brief practice shifts the attention from the individual to the shared being you are arising as together.

Collective Wisdom Circle: Hold sessions focused on intuitive sharing around a specific issue or theme, allowing each participant's insight to emerge naturally.

Model Trust in the Group Field: Regularly acknowledge and affirm moments when the group's shared awareness or wisdom becomes visible.

Facilitate Collective Sensing: Invite participants to listen for what the larger group field is revealing, rather than focusing only on individual perspectives.

Participant Practices

Attune to the Group Being: Practice sensing the presence, mood, or direction of the whole group and share from that awareness.

Deep Listening: Listen deeply to others' insights without interruption or evaluation, supporting the emergence of collective wisdom.

Prompts to Explore Together

- As I slow down and feel the presence of this group, I notice _____.

- If I sense into what we're holding together right now, it feels like _____.

- When I stop trying to understand and simply feel the group, what arises is _____.

- A quiet sense I have about the group today is _____.

- I feel the group most clearly as a whole when _____.

- When I turn toward the shared field we are, I experience _____.

- Something that begins to move in me when I'm just here, with everyone, is _____.

- The energy of this group right now feels _____.

- I sense our shared presence most strongly when _____.

- When we stop speaking and simply rest in the field, I notice _____.

For Individuals (Self-Awareness and Inner Dialogue)

Tuning-In Practice
Each morning, ask, "What does the deeper part of me already know today?" Listen for a felt-sense answer—not a thought, but a quiet awareness. Let this shape how you approach your day.

Field Attunement
Sit in nature or a quiet place. Soften your focus and include everything in your awareness—sounds, sensations, emotions. Ask, "What larger intelligence is moving here, and how am I part of it?" Write about how it feels to include yourself as part of that being rather than separate from it.

Prompts to Explore
- A time today when I felt part of something larger was _____.

- I almost ignored this quiet knowing, but then I felt _____.

- When I listen deeper than my usual thoughts, I sense _____.

- My sense of "higher intelligence" today felt like _____.

Navigating Challenges

Remind groups, and yourself as an individual, to turn toward the higher order of intelligence, especially when individual ideas conflict or seem unclear.

Encourage patience, acknowledging that authentic collective wisdom often emerges slowly and subtly.

Give yourselves time to sit in silence and just be, trusting that opening spaciousness will enable higher intelligence to be known.

Cultivating awareness and acknowledgment of higher intelligence significantly enhances group clarity, creativity, and coherence, guiding groups toward unified action and deeper mutual understanding.

Scenario 1

A marketing team at a mid-sized company is trying to design a campaign for a product launch. They've been in a tense meeting for over an hour, debating logistics and getting nowhere. Ideas are scattered, energy is low, and a sense of pressure dominates the room.

The team leader pauses and says, "Let's take a moment to step back. What if we trusted that something deeper is trying to emerge here, something we don't have to force?" She invites everyone to sit in a minute of quiet, not to solve but to listen—not just to their own ideas, but to the field among them. After this pause, one quieter team member says, "I keep sensing that we're overlooking the emotional story our customers need to feel—maybe we're too focused on tactics." The room shifts. The discussion opens in a new direction, energized, and curious.

Key Insight: By acknowledging a larger intelligence beyond individual minds or roles, the team accesses fresh insight and clarity. The pause allows for receptivity. The group begins to function more like a coherent, sensing organism.

Scenario 2

A multigenerational family is gathered for a holiday dinner. A political comment escalates into a familiar conflict between two siblings. Tension builds, and other family members brace for the usual spiral.

The eldest daughter gently interrupts, "Can we just stop for a second? This moment feels bigger than our opinions. I know we all care about something deeper here. Maybe we could just breathe together for a few seconds." She places her hand on her heart and closes her eyes. A few others follow. The energy begins to shift. After the pause, one brother says, "I don't want to fight. I want us to feel like a family again."

Key Insight: By invoking the presence of something more spacious and unifying—call it love, spirit, or simply the greater field of belonging—the family shifts from reactivity to a more heart-centered state. The interruption of the usual pattern allows a deeper longing to emerge.

Element Four

Articulating Intention

Words are events, they do things, change things. They transform both speaker and hearer; they feed energy back and forth and amplify it.
—*Ursula K. Le Guin*

With this element, we explore the quiet but powerful act of naming what truly matters. Intention is the unseen architecture that shapes how a group feels, moves, and creates together. It forms the atmosphere, focuses the group's energy, and determines what becomes possible. Every group moves on this current—spoken or unspoken, conscious or unconscious. This element invites us to name intention openly, allowing it to be known by all and to offer clarity for the way forward.

Most familiar are the collective intentions around which a group has gathered: What has brought us all together? What are we here to accomplish? While these are often tacit or assumed, the group benefits from remembering them aloud.

Equally important, and uniquely valued in the Eight Elements environment, are our individual intentions. These may shift from meeting to meeting and are rarely voiced. They're often left as quiet hopes. Yet when spoken authentically and received by others, they invite not only actualization but also harmony. A simple pause to ask, "Why am I really here?" brings us into greater alignment with the group and surfaces what we each long to contribute or to receive.

Everyone arrives with different intentions. It's natural. But when they are spoken within the larger shared purpose, something remarkable occurs: Diversity begins to harmonize. Without effort or negotiation, intentions align in surprising ways, creating a coherent field where individual desires naturally support the whole, and vice versa.

This question of intention opens a profound window into unity. It dissolves surface-level roles and expectations, bringing us into a more personal, heartfelt space, which is also where we most easily connect with the larger whole—with the deeper "Why are we here together?" In touching what's most true for ourselves, we often discover the common ground that lives beneath our differences.

Articulating Intention is not about specific goals or polished mission statements. It is about opening a space where the heart of the group can reveal itself. When intentions, whether individual or collective, are given the space to fully emerge, we invite a field of coherence. In that field, alignment arises not through force but through resonance, and what matters most can continue to be present.

How Articulating Intention is Experienced in the Three Groups

Conventional Groups

In Conventional groups, intention is expressed as goals, agendas, and predefined outcomes. It arises from the immediate physical and/or emotional needs of the group and is typically a mental construct—something that's decided in advance and is driven by personal willpower.

The focus is on efficiency and predictability: "What do we need to accomplish today?" or "What's on the agenda?" These intentions tend to be externally imposed or based on familiar roles and routines. Participants may follow them mechanically, without much personal resonance or reflection.

Because intention remains at the surface level, these groups rarely tap into deeper sources of creativity or shared purpose. Conversations can become repetitive, and "groupthink" often dominates. It occurs when individuals go along with prevailing ideas, rather than contributing what is spontaneously arising from their authentic self.

Transitional Groups

In Transitional groups, a shift begins. Intention is no longer just about what needs to get done. It becomes an inquiry into deeper meaning and shared purpose.

Individuals start asking, "What do I long for?" "Why are we really here together?" and "What is possible if we align more fully?"

Intentions in these groups often arise from a personal search for life purpose and are expressed as heartfelt statements or visions. There's an increasing awareness that groups are not only about accomplishing tasks but about becoming something more—places where both personal and collective longings can be explored.

Within organizations, this becomes the territory of corporate purpose, vision, and mission—all vital guides for business success.

While Transitional groups may successfully articulate inspiring intentions, they sometimes struggle to stay connected to them, especially when challenges or emotional tensions arise. The intention is present but may not always be fully embodied. Groups at this stage are learning to return to their shared intentions when things get difficult. They discover how to hold both self-purpose and world purpose in the same space:

- Intention becomes inquiry: "Why are we really here?"

- Individuals begin sharing personal longings and visions.

- More heart-centered, though still learning to stay connected when tensions arise

- Sometimes inspiring but inconsistently embodied

New Wave Groups

In New Wave groups, intention moves beyond something that the mind creates or the group agrees upon. It becomes a living felt presence in the room. Purpose and intention become synonymous and arise spontaneously, as if from the very center of the group's shared being. Individuals feel their personal intentions easily harmonize with something larger. There is a natural impulse to serve the greater good.

Here, intention is experienced as a present-moment imperative—something that calls forth authentic action right now. It doesn't require effort or discussion; it emerges organically through full-hearted expression and deep listening.

In these groups, intention is not a fixed goal but an authentic expression that evolves as the group evolves. Participants sense when the energy drifts. They naturally pause to reconnect with their deeper shared purpose. Rather than being about productivity, these intentions support the evolution of consciousness itself, experienced as "We are here for the benefit of all life."

This is where the group truly becomes a being—one that is alive, awake, and responsive to what is needed in each moment.

Element Four: Articulating Intention

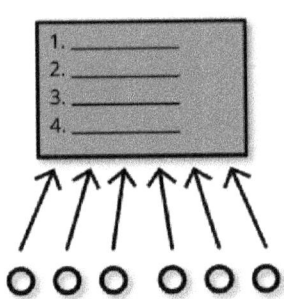
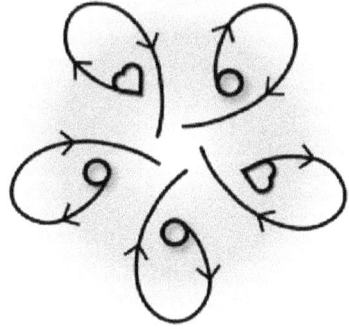
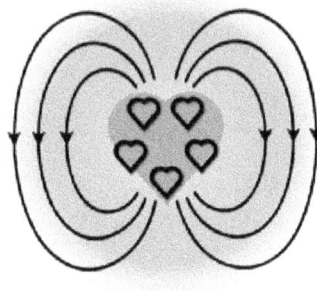

Conventional

Goal setting / agenda

Arises from individual and group physical and emotional needs

Expressed in the form of agenda, goals, structure, modality, etc.

Often a mental construct impelled by self-will

Groupthink

Transitional

Longing / Intention

Arises from a deeper sense of one's life purpose

Known as vision

Sensed as heart's longing

Expressed as a statement of intention

Includes both self-purpose and world purpose

Group becoming

New Wave

Purpose as an imperative

Spontaneous arising of essence from the center of the group whole

The pure arising of each individual's creativity

Expressed as authentic action in the moment

Experienced as being for the benefit of all life, for the purpose of the evolution of life

Full expression from the heart

Group being

Living the Element

You've explored the essence of this element; now comes the invitation to practice it. The sections that follow suggest when it may be most helpful, how it can take shape, and ways to deepen it with those around you.

When to Use

Articulate intention at the very start of any gathering, whether it's a business meeting, a family conversation, a quiet moment with a partner, or a weekend with friends.

Begin with a simple statement of the group's larger purpose. Even if the group's purpose seems obvious, try speaking it aloud anyway. You might be surprised by how much deeper the conversation flows, how naturally connection arises, and how effortlessly the group aligns around what matters most.

After articulating the larger purpose, encourage people to voice their personal intentions—not to shape a collective goal, but simply to be heard and witnessed. You don't need to organize or reconcile these intentions. Trust that by bringing them into the open, a natural alignment will begin to form.

What You Might Say

- Let's turn inward and consider, 'Why am I really here?' and 'What do I most long for at this moment?'

- Articulating intention means openly stating and collectively acknowledging the purpose and goals guiding our group. When we align around a clear intention, our energy becomes focused, harmonious, and powerful, unlocking creativity and deeper connection.

Articulating intention is both a practice and an ongoing commitment. Here are some powerful practices that enable groups to articulate intention clearly and sustainably:

Collective Intention Setting

Begin meetings or gatherings by explicitly stating individual intentions along with the group's larger intention. Invite each participant to express their alignment and personal resonance with that intention to reinforce coherence and collective purpose.

Revisiting and Realignment

Regularly pause to revisit the group's intentions during meetings or collaborative processes, particularly when challenges arise or energies scatter.

Realigning consciously with the articulated intention restores clarity and cohesion.

Intention as Inquiry
Pose questions that invite participants to reflect upon and articulate their deeper intentions regarding their contributions or engagement. These reflective practices foster self-awareness and ensure that intentions remain genuine, heartfelt, and transparent.

The Power of Coherence and Alignment

Clearly articulated intention serves as a powerful unifying force within evolutionary groups. It facilitates coherence and alignment, creating an energetic field capable of holding complexity, fostering creativity, and nurturing collective wisdom. When individuals deeply resonate with a shared intention, their interactions naturally align, harmonizing individual differences into a unified, vibrant, creative whole.

In this unified state, the group can access deeper insights, innovative solutions, and spontaneous creativity. Challenges become opportunities for growth, as participants anchor their responses and interactions in clear, collectively held intentions. Articulating intention significantly enhances the group's capacity for intuitive insight and transformative action.

Exercises and Practical Applications

For Families

Intention Jar
Each family member writes intentions for family time on slips of paper and places them inside a jar. At each gathering, draw one intention, discussing it briefly and setting it as that intention for the time together.

Family Mission Statement

Create a family mission statement together, clearly articulating values, goals, and desired experiences. Include the personal intentions of all family members, as well as those of the group as a whole. Display this mission statement prominently and revisit it monthly to reflect on the group's alignment.

Prompts to Explore Together

Parents

- As parents, our intention in raising our children is _____.

- My personal intention is _____.

- The core value guiding our family decisions is _____.

- We intend to nurture our family's emotional health by _____.

- When conflict arises, our intention is to respond with _____.

- Our ultimate intention for our family's future is _____.

Children

- What I love most about my family is _____.

- Something I'd like our family to do more often is _____.

- I feel happiest at home when _____.

- My wish for my family this year is _____.

- I feel most connected to my family when we _____.

For Businesses

Meeting Intention Check-In

Start each meeting by briefly stating the intended outcome.

Ask participants to verbally confirm their alignment.

Quarterly Intention Retreat
Schedule quarterly off-site meetings dedicated to reviewing and articulating organizational intentions.

Include visioning exercises, collaborative goal setting, and alignment checks.

Prompts to Explore Together
- Our primary intention as an organization is to _____.

- The outcome we intend for this project is _____.

- As a team, we are committed to creating a culture of _____.

- We intend to handle challenges by always focusing on _____.

- Success for us means _____.

- Our shared intention regarding client relationships is _____.

- We will demonstrate alignment with our values by _____.

- Each meeting will begin with the clear intention to _____.

- Our team's guiding principle for decision-making is _____.

- To maintain coherence, we regularly remind ourselves that _____.

For Social Groups

Intentional Gathering Statements
Begin gatherings with playful intention statements (e.g., "Today we intend laughter and connection!").

Group Intention Collage
Create a collective visual collage expressing the group's shared intentions and aspirations.

Regularly update or create new collages as intentions evolve.

Group Reflection

In retrospect, notice any differences in the quality of groups in which you articulated intentions, as compared with those where intentions were not mentioned at all.

Prompts to Explore Together

- We gather as friends with the intention of _____.

- Our time together feels most joyful when we _____.

- One intention I'd love our group to embrace this year is _____.

- Our gatherings become meaningful when we intentionally _____.

- To enhance our group connection, we could try _____.

- We want our group to be known for its commitment to _____.

- Our shared intention when welcoming new members is _____.

- The feeling we most want to create in our gatherings is _____.

- We intentionally support one another by _____.

- Together, our group intends to contribute positively to _____.

For Support / Therapy Groups

Session Intentions Circle

At each session's start, invite members to briefly articulate personal intentions, aligning with the group's supportive environment.

Intentional Healing Journal

Each participant maintains a journal specifically dedicated to recording and reflecting on their healing intentions. Periodically, share selected intentions and insights with the group.

Leader Practices

Intention Setting Ritual: Open meetings by clearly stating intentions.

Regular Alignment Checks: Periodically pause meetings to reaffirm intentions, especially during conflicts or confusion.

Participant Practices
Intention Reflection: Reflect regularly on your personal alignment with the group's intentions, noting insights and areas needing realignment.

Articulate Clearly: Practice expressing personal intentions transparently, contributing to group coherence.

Prompts to Explore Together
- My intention for participating in this group is _____.

- I feel most supported by the group when _____.

- The intention that helps me engage authentically is _____.

- As a group, our shared purpose is to create a space where _____.

- I notice our group's energy feels healthiest when we _____.

- To deepen trust, I intend to practice _____.

- Our intention for group confidentiality is to ensure _____.

- I feel most connected to the group when _____.

- An intention I'd like our group to revisit frequently is _____.

- My personal intention for healing and growth is _____.

For Individuals (Self-Awareness and Inner Dialogue)

One-Sentence Intention
Each morning, complete the sentence, "Today I want to show up with _____." Let it be one quality or orientation (e.g., ease, courage, honesty). Keep it near you as a reminder.

Core Intention Excavation

Reflect on a recurring struggle or pattern. Ask, "What deeper longing is underneath this?" Keep asking, layer by layer, until you reach something simple and essential—like wanting to love, be seen, or rest. Let that become your anchor.

Prompts to Explore

- A core intention I often forget but long to live from is _____.

- When I remember what really matters, I feel _____.

- A surface goal I've been chasing is _____ and underneath that is a longing for _____.

- The quality I most want to bring into my day tomorrow is _____.

Navigating Challenges

Despite its potency, articulating intention can occasionally present challenges. Participants may initially find it difficult to discern or express their deeper intentions clearly. Additionally, group dynamics may shift intentions subtly, requiring careful attention and conscious realignment.

To navigate these challenges, groups can practice patience, clarity, and compassionate inquiry. When misalignment occurs, openly acknowledge it, reaffirming intentions collectively and compassionately. Over time, this process naturally strengthens individual and collective capacities for clarity and coherence.

Ultimately, the intentional practice of articulating and aligning with clear intention transforms group interactions profoundly. It amplifies unity, fosters authenticity, and unlocks immense creative potential. Groups are guided steadily toward deeper self-awareness and unified consciousness.

Scenario 1

A working group has been meeting weekly to redesign an outdated program. The conversation has become scattered and repetitive. One participant says,

"Before we go further, can we each share why we care about this? What brought us into this project?" As people speak, the group hears themes of service, frustration, hope, and care. One member says, "I had no idea we were this aligned underneath it all."

The group decides to write their shared intention at the top of every agenda. Meetings start to feel more focused, energized, and collaborative.

Key Insight: Naming intention brings clarity, alignment, and purpose to a group. It reorients the field around shared meaning, especially when things feel fragmented or task-driven.

Scenario 2

The group has been meeting weekly to organize an upcoming action. Recently, meetings have felt heavy with disagreements, misunderstandings, and fatigue.

One participant speaks up, "Before we dive in today, can we each share why we're here? I think we're losing our shared center." People go around and speak. Some mention systemic change. Others talk about personal healing. One person says they joined to learn how to be part of something bigger.

As intentions are named, the group energy shifts. Conflict softens. There's more curiosity, less urgency. They realize they don't all have the same purpose—but they do share a common ground: the desire to move with care and clarity.

Key Insight: This scenario illustrates how the element of Articulating Intention works in real time—not just to clarify goals, but to highlight where harmonizing the deeper motivations shaping a group field are possible, or even where they are not.

Element Five

Emergence / Letting Nature Lead

Do you have the patience to wait till your mud settles and the water is clear? Can you remain unmoving till the right action arises by itself?
—*Lao Tzu*

This element is about allowing what is truly here, in this moment, to arise—first within each individual. Before anything unfolds in a group, it begins with a simple noticing: What is arising in me right now? A sensation, a feeling, a thought, a spark of intuition—however subtle or unpolished—it is nature moving.

When we allow our inner experience to emerge without judgment or suppression, we are allowing nature to lead through us. This isn't about finding something clever to say or doing what seems appropriate on the surface. It's about staying close to what is deeper, authentic, and alive. The intelligence of life speaks through our real arisings, and as each person allows that emergence, the group field responds.

From there, something larger becomes possible. As individuals allow their true nature to express itself, even if messily, the being of the group begins to come into coherence. And the more the group coheres, the more the group intelligence can inform and deepen what arises in each individual. This is a living, breathing exchange: nature moving as me, as the group, back as me again.

There's no need to steer this process. Emergence doesn't require fixed plans, assigned roles, or predetermined outcomes. It invites presence, receptivity, and trust. When individuals release the need to control or direct the flow and instead attune to what is arising now—within and between them—something more integrated begins to move: a clarity and open-heartedness that grows out of the shared field itself.

Importantly, what arises in us may not always feel comfortable. It may be judgment, anger, confusion, or fear. These, too, are part of nature's unfolding. If we can meet them with honesty and neutrality, speak them without blame, and hold them as part of the group's knowing, they become part of the wisdom that leads us. And even when we can't meet them in that way—when reactivity, pain, or defensiveness takes over—they are still meaningful arisings.

Importantly, uncomfortable arisings mark a place we must move through, not around. These moments often become powerful launch points: The very tension that pulls us into struggle can, when held with care and sincerity, propel us into a very deep healing. And the consciousness that emerges on the other side is often more unified, more loving, and more whole than what came before. This is how emergence happens: not just once, but over and over, moment by moment, through the individuals in the group. In doing so, we're not simply responding to nature—we are nature! And the being of the group becomes not a thing we create, but a living field we participate in, evolve with, and come to know as ourself.

To summarize:

- Emergence begins within the individual—through attending to what authentically arises in the moment.

- That individual emergence is not separate from nature's intelligence; it is nature expressing itself as me.

- When individuals allow that arising, the group field becomes more coherent, and the being of the group evolves.

- Then, the being of the group informs the individuals, and a toroidal movement of co-arising deepens.

- This is not about achieving perfect authenticity, but about being in sincere practice, allowing what arises without forcing or suppression.

- Throughout, we're not controlling or directing—we're sensing what's emerging now, in me, in us, as life.

How Emergence / Letting Nature Lead Is Experienced in the Three Groups

Conventional Groups

In Conventional groups, emergence is often constrained by structure, roles, and expectations. Processes are predefined, and deviations from the plan can be seen as problems. Authentic impulses may arise in individuals, but they're often suppressed in favor of efficiency, hierarchy, protocol, or appropriateness. Spontaneity is rare and can even be viewed as threatening.

In these groups, the natural flow of energy is often overruled by systems of control.

Examples:

- Meetings stick rigidly to agendas or historical patterns, even when a deeper issue is clearly present.

- Emotions or insights that don't "fit" the goal are sidelined or dismissed.

- Team members may feel something's off yet hesitate to speak up.

Transitional Groups

In Transitional groups, there is more openness to emergence but also uncertainty around how to allow it. People may sense something meaningful arising but fall into habits of overtalking, overprocessing, or needing consensus before moving forward. Individuals might share authentic feelings or intuitive hits, although the group hasn't yet built enough trust to fully let go of control. Here, emergence flickers in and out—it's real but not yet reliably trusted.

Examples:

- Someone shares a spontaneous idea, and the group briefly lights up but then returns to "business as usual."

- Participants are aware of emotional undercurrents and are unsure how to hold them.

- The group pauses more often yet still rushes to fill the silence.

New Wave Groups

In New Wave groups, individuals are attuned to what is arising within and know that what emerges carries value, not just for them, but for the whole. Authentic impulses, even when traditionally judged as "messy" or unexpected, are welcomed and sensed as part of a larger field movement. The group isn't waiting for a leader or a plan; it is sensing from within. Emergence flows from the inside out, and the group begins to move as a single living system.

Examples:

- A participant names a subtle inner shift, and the whole group resonates or realigns.

- Silences are trusted as fertile space for something real to arise.

- The group follows threads of insight, emotion, or energy, even when they diverge from the original intent.

Element Five: Emergence / Letting Nature Lead

Conventional	Transitional	New Wave
Similar to childhood	Individuation phase	Adulthood
Dependency on outside authority, such as group leaders, and structure needed to "learn the ropes"	Recognizing and validating self-rhythm, natural wave, needs, and impulses	Spontaneous individual action is an authentic expression of the group
Establishing patterns and learning to depend on what works	Enhancing trust in self-awareness	Meeting and being the arising moment
Socialization, making meaning, and acting from and within norms	Practicing turning toward inner authority at all times	Full individuation allows free flow of core essence and its creativity
	Consciously practicing individuation	
	Turning to and aligning with group while maintaining self-agency and sovereignty	

Living the Element

When to Use

You can turn inward at any moment, in any conversation, by asking yourself, "What is arising in me now?" Emergence is especially helpful when the group is looking for greater authenticity, innovation, or clarity in decision-making, or when you want to deepen interactions and spark creativity. It can also be valuable when things start to feel rigid, forced, or overly structured, as it helps open space for more natural creative flow.

What You Might Say
- Emergence means allowing what is genuinely present in each of us to arise naturally and trusting that by staying close to our real experience, something meaningful begins to move in the group.

- Emergence / Letting Nature Lead invites us to be completely honest and transparent with ourselves and each other. It means openly acknowledging whatever arises in us, even uncomfortable feelings like anger or judgment, without repressing or irresponsibly expressing them. By holding everything neutrally as valuable insight, we allow the group's deeper wisdom to emerge.

Exercises and Practical Applications

For Families

Authenticity Circle
Take turns finishing the sentence: "Right now, I am feeling/experiencing _____."

Simply listen without responding, creating space for genuine sharing.

Emotion Treasure Hunt
Explore difficult emotions by identifying and sharing openly how they offer valuable insights rather than problems to avoid. Invite family members to name a difficult emotion they've felt recently. Ask, "What might this feeling be pointing to? What value or need is it revealing?" Honor each answer without trying to fix or correct.

Prompts to Explore Together
In family settings, emergence often shows up in the unsaid or unexpected—moments when someone changes their mind, expresses a new feeling, or acts out of character. Use these prompts to gently reveal and explore those shifts without pressure to fix or label:

- Something that feels new or different in me today is _____.

- A small moment in our family that surprised me recently was _____.

- When I let myself just be myself, even for a moment, I noticed _____.

- A feeling I didn't expect to have today was _____.

For Businesses

Moment-to-Moment Check-In
Begin a meeting with a quick round of "What's present for you right now?" This is an act of connection and attunement before getting into tasks.

Authentic Innovation Sessions
Hold unstructured sessions where people can voice what's truly working or not, without needing to justify or sugarcoat answers. Let insights arise organically from real, present moment experience.

Prompts to Explore Together
In work environments, emergence can surface as a creative spark, a shift in mood, or the sudden clarity that comes when someone speaks honestly. These prompts help teams slow down and notice what's moving beneath the surface of plans and agendas:

- A fresh idea or impulse I noticed today was _____.

- I almost didn't say this, but I think it matters: _____.

- Something I sensed in the group energy today was _____.

- A moment that felt especially real or unplanned was _____.

For Social Groups

Real Talk Time
Dedicate time in any gathering for spontaneous sharing of what's arising now for each person. No pressure to be profound, just real.

Role-Free Gathering
Host a gathering where members intentionally step out of habitual roles or social scripts and follow what arises moment to moment, whether it's laughter, silence, emotion, or unexpected connection.

Prompts to Explore Together
In social groups, emergence often arrives through humor, silence, awkwardness, or unexpected connection. These prompts bring attention to the aliveness that shows up when people let go of trying to "perform" and simply allow things to unfold:

- A moment when I felt most myself in this group was _____.

- I noticed a shift in energy when _____.

- Something surprising I felt or thought during our time together is _____.

- I didn't expect to say this, but _____.

For Support / Therapy Groups

Authenticity Reflection
Begin with the prompt, "What's authentically here in me right now?" No need to explain or analyze. Just name it.

Neutral Expression Exercise
Invite participants to name emotions or judgments that feel charged. Practice expressing them from a neutral, self-aware stance, acknowledging the energy without directing it at anyone. This also gives participants the opportunity to listen to the statements in neutrality rather than the norm of reactivity.

Prompts to Explore Together
In therapeutic settings, emergence may come through discomfort, vulnerability, or the sense that something deeper is trying to come forward. These prompts honor all states as part of the group's movement toward wholeness:

- A difficult part of me that briefly showed up today was _____.

- I noticed myself holding back when _____.

- An emotion I didn't expect to feel here was _____.

- I'm beginning to sense that underneath my words, there is _____.

For Individuals (Self-Awareness and Inner Dialogue)

Daily Inner Noticing

Set aside 1 minute daily to ask yourself, "What is arising in me right now, without needing to fix it?" Let thoughts, sensations, or impulses appear without interference. Notice any shift in your energy or attention. This builds inner trust and attunement with your personal natural rhythm.

Role-Release Journaling

Write for 20 minutes without structure or goals. Let go of trying to sound wise, complete, or clear. Simply follow what comes next, whether an image, memory, phrase, or blankness. This practice helps loosen the grip of internal roles (i.e., the critic, achiever, helper) and makes space for new, emergent aspects of self to become visible.

Prompts to Explore

- A feeling or thought that surprised me today was _____.

- I almost ignored this part of me, but then I noticed _____.

- A part of me that is shifting or softening lately is _____.

- When I stop trying to figure it out, what starts to come forward is _____.

Navigating Challenges

Emergence can feel enlivening when something fresh and authentic appears, yet it also brings challenges. By its very nature, emergence is unpredictable. What arises may feel awkward, disruptive, or emotionally charged. In moments like these, groups often fall back into old habits—shutting down spontaneity, over-processing, or trying to rush toward clarity.

Common challenges include:

- Discomfort with uncertainty. Silence or ambiguity can be misinterpreted as failure or lack of direction.

- Pressure to produce. Groups may expect emergence to generate polished results quickly, rather than giving it the space to unfold.

- Judgment of what arises. Messy emotions, awkwardness, or unexpected impulses may be suppressed or dismissed.

- Return to control. When things feel risky, individuals or leaders may reassert structure or authority, cutting off the flow.

Ways to meet these challenges:

- Normalize uncertainty. Remind the group that emergence often looks unclear before it feels coherent.

- Pause instead of pushing. When things feel stuck or chaotic, slow down the tempo rather than forcing resolution.

- Treat every arising as meaningful. Even reactivity, silence, or confusion holds information for the group field.

- Trust the process of ripening. Coherence may not appear instantly; it often comes after the group passes through tension or discomfort.

When challenges are met with neutrality and patience, they become thresholds rather than obstacles. What first appears as resistance or breakdown often turns out to be the very material that carries the group into a deeper, more unified field.

Scenario

A group of artists gathers to plan a joint exhibition. The initial meeting is full of ideas, but nothing quite clicks. Deadlines loom. One person finally says, "I don't think we're ready to plan yet. What if we just shared what's alive for us right now—artistically or personally—and see what emerges?"

They go around the circle. Someone speaks of a dream, another shares grief, another laughs unexpectedly. A thread begins to reveal itself: vulnerability, threshold, transformation.

By the end of the session, a theme has arisen organically: "Crossing Points." It feels right to everyone.

Key Insight: When a group loosens control and listens for what is naturally trying to emerge, rather than forcing outcomes, creativity arises. This element honors rhythm, timing, authenticity, self-agency, and organic intelligence.

Element Six

Non-Expert Model / Transparency

There is no teacher, no pupil; there is no leader, no guru. There is only you and your relationship with others and with the world.
— *J. Krishnamurti*

You will see this identical introduction at the beginning of both Elements Six and Seven. That's intentional. These two elements are distinct but inseparable. Each comes more fully alive to the degree the other is active. We recommend reading them together, as thinking of them in tandem will help support a healthy, balanced group field.

The Non-Expert Model and Co-Leadership elements dissolve rigid hierarchies and invite mutual responsibility for the field and all that is created from it.

The Non-Expert Model asks leaders to step out of the role of being the one who knows, releasing the burden of authority and opening the field to the intelligence of the whole. Transparency is how that shift is embodied—by showing up with honesty, humility, and humanity. As this happens, others begin to sense that their own agency is welcome and needed. And as participants step into self-agency—an act of maturity and self-responsibility—the leader is further freed from holding the center alone. This reciprocal movement—stepping back and stepping forward— creates the balanced and mutually trusting environment that allows co-leadership to emerge … the full and natural expression of each person's competence and creativity arising in service of the whole.

Some of the Eight Elements are relatively easy to apply, like pausing for silence or naming an intention. Others ask us to fundamentally shift how we show up in a group—both as participants and as those who hold leadership roles. Elements Six and Seven challenge long-held assumptions about who leads, who follows, and how power and participation are expressed.

Of all Eight Elements, Non-Expert Model / Transparency, and Co-Leadership / Self-Agency may remain especially relevant in educational and structured settings for a long time to come. In contexts where conveying information and supporting skill development in a linear manner are central, considerable expertise and guidance continue to be necessary and appropriate. The shift from conventional to emergent forms of leadership unfolds more gradually here. But even partial movement toward greater transparency and shared responsibility can begin to transform how learning and participation take place, opening the door to deeper, more integrated ways of knowing. These elements help loosen rigid hierarchies without eliminating the value of experience or instruction.

That said, a growing number of educators and educational approaches now focus on awakening the "teacher within" the student, moving toward self-led learning and away from imposed expertise.

Letting Go of the Role of Expert—and Showing Up as an Equal

In Brazil's Kogi tribe, spiritual elders—Mamos—are not "experts" in the Western sense; they are guardians of balance, rather than authorities. Their leadership is based on attunement and humility.

A non-expert group model invites those in visible or implied leadership roles to loosen their grip on needing to know, direct, or appear in control. Instead of leading through expertise alone, they lead through presence.

One of the most powerful shifts a leader can make is to step out from behind the role of "expert" and become a transparent co-participant—one who trusts their own inner wisdom while inviting others to do the same. We believe this kind of self-led awareness is the evolutionary movement needed to meet the complexity of this moment in human history. Groups that embody this shift become spaces where honesty deepens, power balances naturally, and the wisdom and direction needed to move us through this challenging era can more fully have a voice.

When we let go of the need to be the expert who is always certain, and speak openly from our actual experience—our curiosity, our confusion, our care—it creates a field of honesty into which others can relax.

Transparency doesn't mean oversharing or giving away responsibility. It means bringing your whole self forward, not just the polished part. When we do this, we stop reinforcing the distance inherent in hierarchy and begin inviting others into deeper connection. It's an energetic shift—from holding the space alone to inhabiting the space with others.

How Non-Expert Model / Transparency Is Experienced in the Three Groups

Conventional Groups

Leaders are often expected to appear strong, certain, and capable at all times—especially when participants aren't yet self-directed or responsible enough to share leadership. In these situations, showing vulnerability, expressing uncertainty, or admitting "I don't know" can be perceived as weakness and may destabilize the group. Yet, the "expert" role itself can become a mask that limits intimacy and reinforces a power imbalance. Participants may then censor themselves, assuming their contributions are less valid or not really needed.

Transitional Groups

Leaders begin to step down from the pedestal. They experiment with revealing more of their humanness—sharing doubts, questions, or emotions. Transparency may still feel risky or inconsistent, but its impact is felt. It encourages others to relax and express themselves more fully. Power dynamics begin to soften, and connection deepens.

New Wave Groups

Transparency is natural and continuous. There is no need to manage perception. Instead, each person shows up authentically. Leaders become trusted not because they know everything, but because they are real, present, and human. The group becomes a field where everyone feels safe to be seen as they are.

Element Six: Non-Expert Model / Transparency

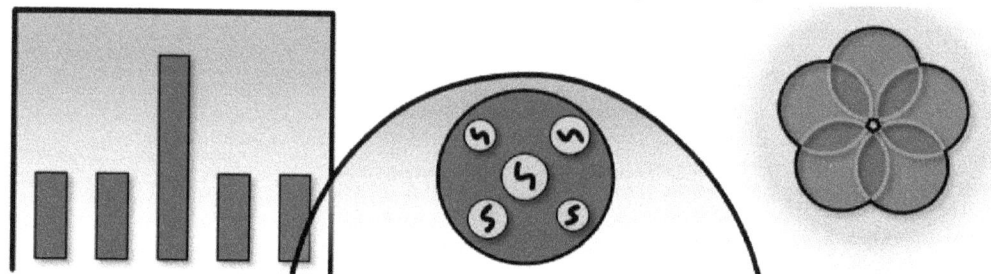

Conventional

Leader not to reveal self, remaining in the "perfect" expert role, as the center of the group

Transparency not really relevant to "getting the job done"

Success of group is considered leader's responsibility

Participants often expected to self-reveal but may be reluctant

Self-revelation enhances separation as one person is focused on more than others

Participants distance themselves from those with whom they don't agree or consider to be "wrong"

Factions or like-minded groups form as individuals self-reveal

Transitional

Leader begins to let more natural personality and essence show, practicing being more present, authentic, and "equal"

Leader steps back / down from holding sole responsibility for success of group

Leader begins to open to shared wisdom from the group participants that reveals because of the less-rigid roles

Participants begin to feel what arises in them when they do not "give themselves away" to an authority (i.e., fears / defenses and joy / healthy power)

New Wave

Each is fully themselves, accepting of all who we are and recognizing that this is the greatest contribution we can make to each other and to the greater good.

Living the Element

You've explored the essence of this element; now comes the invitation to practice it. The sections that follow suggest when it may be most helpful, how it can take shape, and ways to deepen it with those around you.

When to Use

The Non-Expert Model / Transparency often softens tension, breaks performance cycles, and deepens trust. It is especially powerful in the following moments:

- When you feel unpleasant pressure to be the one who knows or holds it all

- When you notice yourself holding back your true experience as a leader

- When you want to foster deeper trust, agency, and participation

- When a moment calls for honesty, not expertise

- When the group members as a whole seem more argumentative or dissatisfied

- When the group energy feels tight, flat, or disengaged

- When participants seem hesitant to speak honestly

- When something vulnerable is arising in you, and you're tempted to hide it

- When there's an overidentification with your role or authority

- When the group needs a shift from performance to presence

What You Might Say

- Transparency means being honest about what's really present—not trying to impress, fix, or control. It's about showing up as a whole human being.

- Practicing the Non-Expert Model means releasing the pressure to lead through knowledge, certainty, or control. Instead, we lead through authenticity—sharing our questions, limitations, and vulnerability as well as our wisdom and talents. This softens hierarchy and opens the space for deeper connection and mutual trust.

Exercises and Practical Applications

For Families

Real Talk Round
During a meal or family moment, each person shares something they're uncertain or curious about—without needing a solution or correction.

Letting Go of Perfection
Everyone reflects aloud on a moment when they felt unsure or made a mistake, and how they moved through it.

Prompts to Explore Together
Parents

- One way I could be more transparent with my children is _____.

- Our family feels more connected when I let go of _____.

- A belief I'm releasing about needing to appear strong all the time is _____.

- I invite trust in our family by showing _____.

- When I am genuinely vulnerable, I notice my child _____.

Children

- I feel closer to my parents when they _____.

- I wish my family knew that sometimes I _____.

- When someone admits they don't know something, I feel _____.

- It helps me feel safe when others share _____.

- I could be more open at home by _____.

For Businesses

Beginning Steps for Leaders to Move Toward Transparency

Owning an Error
Name a recent mistake or misstep of their own, something small but real (e.g., a delay, an overlooked detail, a decision that didn't land well). No self-punishment, just clear acknowledgment. Apologize.

Revealing an Edge
The leader identifies a place where they feel stretched or challenged in a current project—something they are committed to but don't feel fully confident about.

Unpolished Planning
Allow parts of project planning or decision making to happen publicly, in process—not behind closed doors. Share uncertainty and invite input.

Invitations to Partnership
- Here's one assumption I'm making—does anyone see it differently?

- I'll share what's behind my decision making so far; I'd like to hear your reactions.

- This is the trade-off I'm wrestling with—what do you see?

- I'm noticing where I might have blind spots. Where do you think we could look closer?

- Here's what I value most in this decision. What matters most to you?

- Let me be clear about what constraints we're under—and then we can talk about what's possible within them.

Prompts to Explore Together
- One way I can show up more transparently at work is _____.

- When a leader shares openly, I feel _____.

- What I don't want my team to see about me is _____.

- When someone on my team shows vulnerability, I feel _____.

- One belief I could release about professional "expertise" is _____.

For Social Groups

What's Real?
Open a gathering with the question, "What's most real for you right now?" Each person responds briefly, without discussion.

If you often host or lead social spaces, take a moment to share something genuine—not just gratitude or logistics, but something honest and vulnerable.

Prompts to Explore Together
- I feel closest to people who _____.

- When I'm not trying to be impressive, I _____.

- Our group energy shifts when someone reveals _____.

- I appreciate it when someone says _____.

- One way I could support more openness in this group is by _____.

For Support / Therapy Groups

Leader Vulnerability
Occasionally name a moment of real feeling or reflection.

Transparency Pairs
Pair up for 5-minute shares about a current inner challenge or uncertainty. The listener simply receives, without comment, response, or fixing.

Prompts to Explore Together

- When someone shares something vulnerable, I usually feel _____.

- A moment when I felt safe in this group was when _____.

- I want to practice sharing more honestly about _____.

- Transparency, to me, feels like _____.

- I could bring more of myself to the group by _____.

Leader Practices

Release the need to perform. Practice naming your real experience without apology or overexplanation.

Model moments of "I don't know," or "I'm noticing...," to open space.

Invite others to share from their lived experience, rather than from their expertise.

Watch for projections of authority—and gently redirect the group toward shared wisdom.

Participant Practices

Notice when you hold back out of fear of being wrong or imperfect.

Share something unfinished, emotional, or true.

Reflect on how it feels to hear transparency in others—and whether you allow yourself that same freedom.

Trust that your vulnerability may open the door for someone else.

For Individuals (Self-Awareness and Inner Dialogue)

Reveal to Yourself
Pause once a day to ask: "What am I pretending not to know or feel?" Let the answer emerge gently. You don't have to judge, fix, or share it—just be honest with yourself.

Transparent Journaling
Write a private journal entry as if no one will ever read it. Let go of performing, explaining, or framing things positively. Let yourself speak transparently from the parts you usually hide. Afterward, reflect, "What part of me needed to be heard?"

Prompts to Explore
- Something about myself I don't want anyone to see is _____.
- When I'm fully honest with myself, I see _____.
- A truth I often downplay, but feel strongly, is _____.
- If I didn't have to be the expert in my own life, I would feel _____.

Build slowly. Safety deepens over time. One real moment is often enough to shift the whole atmosphere.

By stepping out of the expert role and into real presence, we create an environment where everyone can be more human, more whole, and more connected. Transparency isn't about being perfect—it's about being real and supporting others to do the same.

Scenario 1

A long-time facilitator is leading a group on collaborative leadership. Midway through, someone challenges her framing. She feels heat rise in her chest. Her usual instinct would be to defend or redirect.

Instead, she pauses and says, "I notice I want to have the perfect answer right now—and I don't. I'm sitting with your question. Let's all feel into it."

The room quiets. Far from diminishing her authority, her honesty deepens the trust in the room. Other participants begin sharing more openly, too.

Key Insight: When a leader or anyone models transparency, it invites authenticity across the group. The need to know or fix gives way to real presence, allowing deeper wisdom to enter.

Scenario 2

Here's an example of how to apply the Non-Expert Model to the group of inner voices—the "committee" many people experience within:

Robert is wrestling with a decision—whether to accept a speaking invitation that feels both exciting and intimidating. Inside, a familiar cast of voices appears:

- The Planner says, "Let's be strategic. This could be good visibility."

- The Inner Critic warns, "You'll mess it up. You're not polished enough."

- The Idealist chimes in, "Say yes! You have to serve the greater good."

- The Worried Child whispers, "What if everyone hates it?"

In the past, Robert would let the Planner or the Idealist take charge, dismissing the others as distractions. But this time, he pauses. He recognizes that trying to identify which voice is "right" just reenacts a hierarchy. He decides to apply the Non-Expert Model.

He gently lets each voice speak fully, without rushing to fix, silence, or override any of them. Instead of seeking the "correct" answer from one dominant voice, he listens for what truth each voice is carrying—what it longs for, what it protects.

As he does, something softens. The Critic reveals a fear of being humiliated. The Idealist admits it wants meaning, not just performance. Even the Planner wants him to feel resourced, not just strategic.

By releasing the idea that any one voice is the expert, a deeper intelligence begins to surface from the space between them rather than from any individual part. A quiet clarity arises outside of the usual decision-making process. Robert sees how to move forward in a way that feels whole.

Key Insight: When we stop searching for the "right" voice and instead welcome each part of ourselves as a valid expression of care or longing, a wiser coherence emerges. The Non-Expert Model shows that wholeness doesn't come from one perspective winning, but from honoring the truth in all of them and letting a larger intelligence arise from their conversation.

Element Seven

Co-Leadership / Self-Agency

*There is no teacher, no pupil; there is no leader, no guru. There is
only you and your relationship with others and with the world.*
—*J. Krishnamurti*

You will see this identical introduction at the beginning of both Elements Six and Seven. That's intentional. These two elements are distinct but inseparable. Each comes more fully alive to the degree the other is active. We recommend reading them together, as thinking of them in tandem will help support a healthy, balanced group field.

The Non-Expert Model and Co-Leadership elements dissolve rigid hierarchies and invite mutual responsibility for the field and all that is created from it.

The Non-Expert Model asks leaders to step out of the role of being the one who knows, releasing the burden of authority and opening the field to the intelligence of the whole. Transparency is how that shift is embodied—by showing up with honesty, humility, and humanity. As this happens, others begin to sense that their own agency is welcome and needed. And as participants step into self-agency—an act of maturity and self-responsibility—the leader is further freed from holding the center alone. This reciprocal movement—stepping back and stepping forward— creates the balanced and mutually trusting environment that allows co-leadership to emerge ... the full and natural expression of each person's competence and creativity arising in service of the whole.

Some of the Eight Elements are relatively easy to apply like pausing for silence or naming an intention. Others ask us to fundamentally shift how we show up in a group—both as participants and as those who hold leadership roles. Elements Six and Seven challenge long-held assumptions about who leads, who follows, and how power and participation are expressed.

Of all Eight Elements, Non-Expert Model / Transparency and Co-Leadership / Self-Agency may remain especially relevant in educational and structured settings for a long time to come. In contexts where conveying information and supporting skill development in a linear manner are central, considerable expertise and guidance continue to be necessary and appropriate. The shift from conventional to emergent forms of leadership unfolds more gradually here—but even partial movement toward greater transparency and shared responsibility can begin to transform how learning and participation take place, opening the door to deeper, more integrated ways of knowing. These elements help loosen rigid hierarchies, without eliminating the value of experience or instruction.

That said, a growing number of educators and educational approaches now focus on awakening the "teacher within" the student, moving toward self-led learning and away from imposed expertise.

Co-Leadership / Self-Agency

In these chaotic and rapidly shifting times, the most essential capacity we can develop is the ability to sense what unique strengths lie within us and to act from that place, even when it feels subtle or incomplete. Self-agency, grounded in this kind of inner attunement, becomes a stabilizing force in the face of uncertainty. As external systems fragment, our capacity to act from our internal alignment, without waiting for permission or deferring to external authority, becomes essential.

Element Seven invites us to dissolve the traditional boundaries between leader and participant by inviting the full self-agency of every individual in the group. This isn't about everyone taking turns being in charge. It's about stepping into mutual ownership of the group, leading from within, not from above.

When one steps into co-leadership, participants no longer depend on someone else to set the tone, hold the structure, or define what's valuable. Leadership isn't a role but a living dynamic. Each person participates as an equal carrier of the group's intelligence, empowered to contribute from their own wisdom, integrity and essence. Everyone recognizes that their unique expression is both needed and welcome.

Self-agency is the inner movement from passivity to participation, from following to initiating, from waiting to owning. It's the recognition that no one else can bring what you can. It isn't dominating or controlling. It's acting from your own clarity, attunement, and care for the whole. It means all participants attend to and are responsible for the whole as well as for themselves.

When self-agency becomes active across a group, leadership shifts. It moves out of a fixed role and becomes a shared quality—a felt field that anyone can embody in any moment. This is co-leadership: not a title or position, but a dynamic, emergent way of holding the group from within.

How Co-Leadership / Self-Agency Is Experienced in the Three Groups

Conventional Groups

Fullest self-expression comes from the leader, though even that may be limited.

Participants' expressions fall within norms or expectations.

Most follow or defer to the leader's direction.

Outcomes are generally predictable and contained within a known range.

Transitional Groups

Participants and leaders are moving toward more authentic, spontaneous expression.

Everyone encounters resistance to fuller presence but works through it.

The group becomes a source of encouragement and reflection.

Each person begins to claim responsibility for the group field.

There's a growing sense of mystery, aliveness, and creative possibility.

New Wave Groups

The group expresses itself through the full authenticity and talent of every member.

Each individual is an actualized self-responsible carrier of the group's wholeness.

Leadership is shared fluidly, presence and intuition guide participation.

The group becomes a coherent vessel for higher intelligence.

What emerges is often unexpected, deeply resonant, and entirely co-created.

Element Seven: Co-Leadership / Self Agency

Conventional

Fullest self-expression is by leader, although somewhat limited to maintain role and position

Participants follow and defer to leader

Participants' expressions fall within a norm

Results somewhat predictable or expected within a range of possibility

Transitional

Participants (and leader) moving toward more authentic, unique, and spontaneous expression

New Wave

Each person fully actualized and self-responsible owner of entire group

Full self-expression of group body through expression of essence and talent of each participant

Fullest expression of higher intelligence

Unimagined creation!

Living the Element

When to Use

Turning toward Co-Leadership / Self-Agency can shift a group from dependency to vitality. It's especially useful when:

- A group is relying too heavily on one leader or facilitator

- A few people dominate while others hold back

- You feel something important is missing—and sense that it might be you

- You notice yourself hesitating to contribute, waiting for permission or clarity

- You want the group to feel more like a shared experience than a performance

- The energy feels flat, overstructured, or disconnected

What You Might Say

- In this space, we're not relying on one person to lead or hold all the wisdom. Instead, we're practicing something a little different—what we call co-leadership. That means each of us is invited to bring our own attention, insight, and presence to the group. You don't need to wait for permission to speak what feels true or to notice something important.

- It's not about taking over—it's about sensing when something in you wants to participate and trusting that your expression matters. If you feel a tug to ask a question, to slow us down, or to offer something you're noticing, that's a form of leadership. When each person listens and contributes from that place, something greater than any one of us starts to come forward.

- In this group, leadership isn't fixed—it arises. At any moment, any one of us may feel the call to offer a reflection, name a shift in energy, or guide our attention in a new direction. That's not just welcomed—it's essential.

- We're not looking for someone to steer or decide; we're cultivating an environment where self-agency and mutual trust allow the group itself to lead. That means you might feel moved to initiate something or to sense when it's time to pause. You might even notice when you're holding back, and in this environment, that noticing is leadership.

- We're practicing the art of leading and following simultaneously, with each of us attuned to what wants to arise through the whole and trusting ourselves to be the voice through which the higher self of the group is speaking at the moment.

Exercises and Practical Applications

Transparency Moment

In your next group interaction, notice an opportunity where you might normally withhold something: a question, a doubt, an emotion, or a truth. Try sharing it gently and clearly. Then observe how the group energy shifts.

Self-Agency Observation

For 1 week, observe whether the comments and actions in your groups arise from self-agency, or from deferral, expectation, or habit. Are you supporting another's agency with your presence?

Take a Turn, Then Step Back

Try initiating something in your group—a direction, a comment, an energetic tone—and then consciously step back to let others shape what comes next. Watch what emerges.

Practice "Being Equal"

In any group such as family, work, or with friends, try perceiving yourself not as "above" or "below" anyone, but as a fully equal part of the field. See how this shifts your participation.

Reflection Questions

In what situations do you feel most comfortable being transparent? Where do you hold back?

When has someone's vulnerability allowed you to show more of yourself?

What does self-agency feel like in your body?

Do you tend to defer to others in group settings, or do you dominate? What might it look like to balance that?

What's one thing you might say in your next group meeting that would be more transparent or self-authored?

Can you identify a moment in a group where co-leadership spontaneously emerged?

What would shift if you fully believed your voice, your energy, and your presence matter in every group you're in?

For Families

Ownership Moments
Invite each family member to take responsibility for something that serves the whole, such as an activity, a tone, a check-in, or a transition.

Shared-Day Design
Let each person design one part of the day or week for the family. Create space for each unique style of care and leadership.

Prompts to Explore Together
Parents
- One way I can let my child take more ownership is _____.

- Our family feels more balanced when _____.

- I notice agency in my child when they _____.

- I'm practicing stepping back by _____.

Children
- I feel proud when I _____ for our family.

- When I take the lead on something, I feel _____.

- One thing I'd like to take charge of is _____.

- I feel more part of our family when _____.

For Businesses

Responsibility Round
At the start of meetings, invite each team member to name one thing they're taking full ownership of this week—practical or energetic.

Peer-Led Sessions
Rotate who leads check-ins, agendas, or brainstorming, regardless of title or department.

Prompts to Explore Together
- A place I could step into more self-agency is _____.

- I hold back when _____.

- When I initiate from my own clarity, I notice _____.

- Our team feels most alive when _____.

- We could support shared leadership better by _____.

For Social Groups

Rotating Roles
Let hosting, guiding, or facilitating rotate naturally. Invite everyone to try a new role.

Moment of Initiative
Practice sensing when something is needed. Name, offer, or initiate it without waiting for the usual leader.

Prompts to Explore Together

- A time I stepped into leadership in this group was when _____.

- I feel energized to contribute when _____.

- We become more creative when _____.

- One way I can help balance energy in the group is by _____.

- I'd love to offer _____ to this group.

For Support / Therapy Groups

Speak to the Field
Encourage group members to speak from a sense of what they feel is needed in the whole, not just their own story.

Shared Holding Practice
Temporarily remove the facilitator's central role. Let the group self-organize and reflect on what it feels like to share the container.

Prompts to Explore Together

- I experience my own agency in the group when I _____.

- I feel safer contributing when _____.

- A moment I led from presence was when _____.

- This group feels strongest when _____.

- I could offer more to the group by _____.

Leader Practices
Pause often and ask, "Who else feels moved to carry this?"

Notice if you are holding more than is necessary and gently step back.

Celebrate when someone steps into leadership, however briefly.

Reflect regularly, "What kind of leadership is emerging here? Is it shared?"

Model leading from alignment instead of authority.

Participant Practices

Trust your impulse to speak, offer, or shift the tone.

Notice what feels alive in you and bring it forward with care.

Ask yourself, "What am I sensing the group needs, and what part can I hold?"

Stay responsive, not reactive. Lead from presence and not pressure.

Encourage others to step forward by making space and listening deeply.

For Individuals (Self-Awareness and Inner Dialogue)

Inner Leadership Check-In

Each morning, ask, "Where do I want to take more responsibility today?" Pick one small area: your attention, tone, or pacing. Lead yourself with care.

Inner Co-Agency Map

Draw a map of "voices" or roles inside you, such as the planner, critic, dreamer, or peacemaker. Identify which ones tend to lead. Then ask, "Which voice do I want to empower now?" Practice letting new voices lead while honoring the others.

Prompts to Explore

- A place where I tend to give up my own agency is _____.

- Today, I took the lead in my own life by _____.

- A part of me I want to trust more deeply is _____.

- Leadership, in my inner life, means _____.

Navigating Challenges

Self-agency can feel risky. Practice in small, meaningful ways.

Not everyone will lead the same way—honor diverse forms of contribution. Group patterns may resist change at first but stay with it.

Co-leadership doesn't mean no structure—it means shared responsibility. Be gentle with yourself and others. This is a cultural shift, not just a skill.

Closing Invitation

As we become more sensitive to what unites and what fragments, we may feel the flatness of roles, the tension of control, the ache of unexpressed truth. In those moments, consider this:

- What would it be like to show more of myself here?

- What would it be like to trust the group to carry what arises?

- What would it be like if no one were "in charge," but everyone was fully present?

- Co-leadership is not a technique but an evolutionary shift in how we relate. It's a return to inner sovereignty, trust in the group field, and a practice of freedom.

Scenario 1

In a peer-led creative circle, a long-time member notices that one participant has been unusually quiet for several meetings. He waits, sensing into the group, then says, "I just want to name that I've been noticing you, Jordan, and wonder if there's something we're not making room for."

Jordan pauses, then speaks, "Thank you. I wasn't sure how to say it, but I've felt pretty invisible here lately."

What follows is one of the most honest conversations the group has had in months. Not because it was facilitated from the front, but because someone led from within.

Key Insight: Self-agency doesn't always look like taking charge. It can look like naming what's true, offering what's needed, or initiating a shift in tone. When group members step into this kind of presence, the group becomes more sensitive, honest, and whole.

Scenario 2

A support group has been meeting weekly for many years with the same facilitator who is a skilled and compassionate leader whom everyone trusts. Over time, the group has become close-knit, and participants feel increasingly confident in their presence and contributions.

One evening, as the facilitator is about to guide the usual closing round, a participant gently speaks up: "Would it be okay if we tried something a little different tonight? I was thinking we could each offer a word or phrase that captures how we're leaving, and maybe someone else could close us out instead of you—just to see what that feels like."

The facilitator pauses, sensing the sincerity, and care behind the suggestion. He nods, surprised but open. Another group member offers to facilitate the closing, and the group flows into a new rhythm. There's a quiet aliveness in the room; something subtle has shifted. The facilitator still holds the container, but now others are beginning to shape it too.

The following week, the facilitator arrives with something quietly new in his tone. After welcoming everyone, he says, "Would anyone like to lead the opening tonight—with a question, a tone, a moment of silence ... whatever feels right?"

There's a pause. One participant smiles and offers a short centering breath for the group.

After the opening, the facilitator adds, "I've been reflecting on last week and how someone stepped forward to suggest a new way of closing. Let's take some time tonight to talk about this ... about self-agency ... and how we each sense it beginning to arise in this group. What feels possible now, and what kind of shared leadership might be wanting to unfold?"

Key Insight: Co-leadership doesn't require dismantling structure all at once. It begins with noticing when energy starts to shift and responding with openness. When a leader makes space for participants to step forward, and when participants sense they have space to offer more, the group begins to move from a leader-centered model toward a living field of shared responsibility. Co-leadership is not imposed; it arises when the group starts to trust its own intelligence.

Element Eight

Attending to Frequency / Connection

Where the higher flows into the lower, it transforms
the nature of the lower into that of the higher.
—*Meister Eckhart*

Never doubt that a small group of thoughtful, committed citizens
can change the world. Indeed, it is the only thing that ever has.
—*Margaret Mead*

Frequency is the subtle energetic quality that arises from and shapes our interactions and experience.

Connection is how deeply and harmoniously we experience each other and are present for each other and for ourselves.

As we move toward more unitive awareness, frequency and connection are inseparable. Each one evokes the other. When the frequency is coherent, connection deepens. When connection is real and mutual, the frequency rises. This interplay is subtle but tangible, and when we learn to sense it, we gain access to a powerful source of group well-being.

The element of Attending to Frequency / Connection invites us to sense what often goes unnoticed and almost always unspoken: the vibrational quality of the group field. Every group has a frequency—an energetic tone shaped by our bodies, thoughts, emotions, and intentions. At the same time, this frequency is deeply impacted by connection—how attuned we are to one another, how seen and received we feel, and how safely we sense we can be ourselves.

This frequency can show up in many ways, depending on what is present in the group:

- Low-frequency states like fear, pressure, or judgment accompany fragmented relationships.

- High-frequency states like presence, mutuality, and open-heartedness foster coherence and creative flow.

When we attend to frequency and connection, we care for the invisible structure that holds the group. This isn't about managing mood or avoiding discomfort. It's about tending to the integrity of the field itself, and being fully present with whatever is arising. Without this care, even well-intentioned groups can lose their spark or drift apart. With it, a group becomes much more than the sum of its parts.

We know the frequency and connection of a group not through analysis, but by sensing them. They're subtle but real qualities like the emotional tone in the room or the "weather" of the shared field. You might feel it in your body as a sense of ease, openness, and aliveness when the group is connected and the frequency is high, or as a tightness, restlessness, boredom, or distraction when it's low.

Aligned groups often feel spacious, attuned, quietly joyful. There's a natural rhythm—a sense of being both relaxed and engaged. People listen more fully, speak more easily and truthfully. Even silence feels rich.

When the frequency drops, the opposite tends to arise: disconnection, overtalking, zoning out, tension, or a sense of pressure or fog. These shifts can be subtle, but they're noticeable when we pause and tune in. Learning to sense them, without judgment, gives us the ability to tend to the group field in real time, helping it return to wholeness when it fragments, and savoring it when it's in flow.

How Attending to Frequency / Connection Is Experienced in the Three Groups

Conventional Groups

Reliance on external rules, norms, or control assures acceptable group behavior and maintains order. The idea of sensing frequency or connection may feel unfamiliar or unnecessary. Dissonance is addressed through authority or redirection, rather than enhanced awareness. Coherence is randomly achieved and rarely held as a goal.

Transitional Groups

Transitional groups begin to notice the effects of group energy and interpersonal connection. Tools like check-ins, facilitation techniques, or emotional processing may be used, but these efforts are often still externally guided, rather than arising organically from group attunement.

New Wave Groups

A New Wave group recognizes the group as a living being. Frequency and connection are sensed and stewarded, moment by moment. Adjustments happen naturally through honesty, humor, silence, or by simply listening. The group moves fluidly, aligned from within. Connection is much more than interpersonal bonding—it's a felt sense of being part of a unified, living whole.

Element Eight: Attending to Frequency / Connection

Conventional	Transitional	New Wave
Responsibility of the leader to manage the group "vibe"	Exploration of frequency, coherence, and connection and their value as signposts to unitive awareness	High-frequency coherence, synchronicity
Connection of the group members also responsibility of leader and often conditional	Recognition that connection is far more important, potent, and healing than content	Connection is inherent, unconditional, and maintained by in-the-moment authenticity
Information and story are prerequisites to connection	Intimacy and connection are functions of being truthful in the moment	Full expression of heart
Coherence randomly achieved and not consciously worked toward		
Mind over heart		

Living the Element

When to Use

Attending to Frequency / Connection is especially useful:

- When something in the group feels "off" but isn't easy, or even possible, to name

- When the energy drops and things feel flat or fragmented

- When there's tension, tiredness, withdrawal, boredom, or disconnection

119

- When you want to deepen presence, attunement, or joy

- When things are going well and you want to sustain or amplify the sense of flow

- When your group is moving into something new and needs a reset

- Any time you want to feel more connected—to self, each other, and the being of the group

What You Might Say

- Let's take a moment to sense the atmosphere here—not just what's being said, but how it feels to be together. Is there tension? Ease? Energy? Disconnection?

- Frequency is the energetic quality of our presence—how we're showing up emotionally, mentally, even subtly. It's the vibe. Connection is how attuned we are to ourselves, to one another, and to the field we share.

- Let's take a moment to notice: What's the overall tone here? Is it light, charged, sluggish, warm? What's happening in the space among us? How connected do you feel to yourself and to the group?

- Attending to this shared field lets us move from unconscious habits to conscious coherence, where alignment, repair, and deeper listening become possible.

- Notice all your senses. What are you experiencing?

- Let's pause and notice the atmosphere in the room. We don't need to fix anything—just sense and name what's here for each of us.

- We all know when something feels off or disconnected in a group, even if we don't have words for it. This element invites us to pay attention to those subtle shifts. The frequency of the group—the vibe, the tone, the atmosphere—impacts how we connect, how we feel, and what becomes possible here.

- This isn't about making everything positive or smooth. It's about honestly sensing what's happening in the group field and tending to it with care, just as we would tend a living garden or a shared space.

- Let's try something different: instead of analyzing where we are stuck, let's feel into the quality of our connection and the energy we're creating together. Sometimes, tending to that shifts everything else.

In summary …

This element is often the one that brings everything else together. It's how we sustain the coherence we've cultivated. It's how we begin again when things unravel. It's how we keep the group field alive, aligned, and open to new possibilities.

When in doubt, tune in to the frequency. When you're unsure what's needed, turn toward connection. They will show you.

A Note of Care

As we tune in to frequency and connection, it's important not to assume we know what someone else is feeling or intending. Energy can be subtle; it is shaped by our own projections or past experiences. If something feels off, let it be an invitation to curiosity, not conclusion.

Do not assume. Ask, check in, clarify. Let your senses serve connection, not separation. Only the other can truly tell you what's going on inside them.

And remember: We each make meaning differently. Even shared words or gestures can land in wildly different ways. Don't assume others interpret things the way you do—remain open and let understanding be something you build together.

Sensing Frequency: How to Tell When Something Feels Off or in Flow and What to Do About It

Now you know when to pay attention to the element. But how exactly do you do that?

We don't figure out group frequency with the mind. We sense it with the whole being. All of us are built to perceive subtle shifts in energy. The key is being aware of the signals your system is already receiving.

In this chapter, we turn our attention to the less familiar senses—the subtler, higher-frequency layers of perception that aren't usually named or identified. In her classic 1987 book, *Hands of Light*, Barbara Ann Brennan describes what she calls a "high Sense" component to our five ordinarily recognized senses, extending sight, hearing, touch, taste, and smell into more refined dimensions. She also names additional senses beyond the usual five, expanding the ways we can register information. Together, these expanded and heightened senses can help us attune to the group field with greater clarity and depth. They allow us not only to notice when something feels off, but also to recognize and savor when things are flowing, connected, and alive.

Everyone senses differently. Some of us feel things strongly in our bodies. Others are more visual, auditory, or emotionally attuned. Frequency awareness is about becoming honest and present with what your system is already noticing.

Sense One: Kinesthetic (i.e., Body Movement and Sensation)
This is your physically felt sense of energy and movement.

Examples:
In a high-frequency group, your posture may relax and your breath settle into an easy rhythm. You may even sense a pleasant current moving through your limbs. At lower-frequency moments, you might cross your arms, feel an urge to move away, breathe more shallowly, or notice tightness in your chest or jaw.

Actions to elevate the frequency

Move! Do anything that will free up some of the energy held in your body. Stretch. Breathe. Burp. Yell. Sing. Dance. Anything. Just Move!

Sense Two: Personal Emotions (i.e., Mad, Glad, Sad, Fearful)

This is your awareness of any emotion present for you in the moment.

Examples:

In high-frequency spaces, you might feel glad or moved. In lower-frequency moments, you may be shut down or may notice irritation, fear, or sudden sadness without a clear reason. Often, the group field is carrying something that hasn't yet been named.

Actions to elevate frequency and deepen connection

Be truthful with yourself and others. When we name what's true without projecting it onto another, we create space for deeper resonance and connection. No fixing or blaming, simply being real and present.

Speak your truth with care, offering your feelings as a way of being known and letting others be with you. When being honest, we allow the group to recalibrate around something real.

What lowers the group's frequency and leads to separation isn't the feeling itself, it's the suppression, denial, or unconscious acting out of that feeling.

Emotions we sometimes label as "difficult" or "negative" aren't bad or wrong—they are part of life, part of being human. When expressed with self-responsibility, they are passageways to higher frequency and deeper connection. Honesty raises the frequency; as frequency rises, connection is enhanced.

Sense Three: Intuition (i.e., The Subtle Inner Sense)

This is your quiet knowing beneath the surface of thought. It is an instinctive feeling, without the need for conscious reasoning.

Examples:
You walk into a room and instantly feel tension—even though no one has spoken. You sense the group is avoiding something. Or you feel inexplicably uplifted and safe, without knowing exactly why. Even the silence feels rich and inviting.

Actions to elevate frequency and deepen connection
When something feels off—or beautifully right—and you just know, don't dismiss it. Intuition often picks up shifts in the group field before they're visible or verbalized. Trust it enough to pause, reflect, and if appropriate, name it with care. These small intuitive acknowledgments help the group orient around subtle truth and open space for others to share.

The key is curiosity, not certainty. You're simply articulating your inner awareness as one thread in the group's unfolding tapestry. When offered with humility and openness, intuitive sensing becomes a powerful way to lift the field into greater coherence.

Sense Four: Experiencing Love for Others (i.e., Relational Warmth and Openness)
This sense lets you feel the heart connection between yourself and others.

Examples:
In attuned groups, you may feel a surge of compassion, quiet appreciation, or the desire to include others. When frequency drops, you may notice withdrawal, judgment, or numbness toward others, even if you don't know why. While heart connection need not be interrupted when there's a drop in frequency, we often unconsciously pull back from others as a learned childhood defense against pain.

Actions to elevate frequency and deepen connection
Notice when you feel disconnected and simply choose to open your heart a little more.

When you sense warmth, tenderness, or quiet care for others in the group, even just a flicker, let yourself feel it. This subtle sense of love or affection is the energetic glue that holds groups in resonance and coherence.

Love is often purely a gentle presence, appreciation, or stillness. When we allow ourselves to feel it and share it in simple, selfless ways, it infuses the group with safety, humanity, and aliveness.

Let your actions carry the feeling, listen more deeply, offer a wordless smile, hold space without rushing in to fix.

Senses Five, Six, and Seven: Hearing, Taste, and Smell (i.e., Subtle and Physical Cues)

These senses give us subtle, often unconscious, cues about the group field. They inform us of the tone, vitality, and coherence of a group, not through logic or expectation, but through the texture of experience.

Hearing

This sense helps us attune to how things are being said, not just what is said.

Examples:

In coherent fields, speech has rhythm, flow, and warmth, and even silence feels full. In a discordant space, you may hear rushed words, long gaps, or an urge to interrupt. The "tone" of the group is often more revealing than the content.

Actions to elevate frequency and deepen connection

Speak with presence. Let your voice reflect calm and care. A grounded tone often soothes a jagged field. Invite awareness. Listen beneath the words for emotions or unspoken needs carried by the tone.

When speech becomes more conscious, frequency rises. The group field becomes clearer, more resonant, more human.

Taste

Taste symbolizes the emotional flavor of an interaction or space.

Examples:

Some people feel a metallic taste when tension arises or experience "sweetness" when connection deepens.

Actions to elevate frequency

Notice if your mouth is dry, tight, or suddenly bitter. These can be signs that something needs attention in the group field. Use breath, water, or a mint to reset your own inner tone and bring freshness back into the moment.

Taste may be subtle, but it helps us recognize when something is "hard to swallow" or when we're truly digesting the experience together.

Smell

The sense of smell registers the atmosphere—both literally and energetically.

Examples:

While often subtle, we may notice when a space smells "stale," "heavy," "clean," or "charged."

Actions to elevate frequency

Change the energetic scent: Freshen the air, turn on an air purifier, open a window, light a candle (making sure there is a flow of fresh air), bring in something natural like flowers and herbs, or use essential oils. You can also "clear the space" through intentional awareness, silence, or breath. The sense of smell reminds us that the group field, like a room, needs ventilation and care.

Sense Eight: Vision (i.e., Outer and Inner Sight)

This sense also is both physical and subtle. With outward sight, we notice faces, gestures, and movements—how someone's eyes brighten, a body leans in, or the whole group visibly relaxes. These visible cues give us a read on the tone and vitality of the moment.

Inward sight is quieter. It's the sense of seeing with the "inner eye"—the viewing of images, colors, or impressions that arise when you close your eyes or soften your gaze. Sometimes, the group may appear in your imagination as cloudy or dim,

126

other times bright, flowing, or spacious. This isn't about predicting or analyzing but simply letting yourself perceive what the field looks like to you.

Examples:

In high-frequency moments, faces appear more radiant, postures open, and the whole space looks luminous. Inwardly, you might sense light, color, or movement.

In lower-frequency moments, you may see slumped shoulders, darting eyes, or closed expressions. Inwardly, the field may appear dull, stagnant, or constricted.

Actions to elevate frequency and deepen connection

Soften your gaze and take in the whole field, rather than focusing only on individuals. This widens awareness and supports coherence.

Experiment with closing your eyes briefly, sensing the "look" of the group inwardly, and then reopening them to compare inner and outer vision.

Name what you notice gently: "I see we all seem a bit tense right now" or "I'm seeing more openness in our faces." Simple observations can bring the unseen into awareness and help the group recalibrate.

If things feel flat or closed, shift the visual field: light a candle, move seats, open curtains. Small visual changes refresh perception and can subtly lift the group's tone.

Sense Nine: Direct Knowing

This is often the clearest and most unfiltered sense. It doesn't come through image, sound, or body. You simply know—a sudden clarity about what's going on, even if you can't explain how.

Examples:

A fully formed, lengthy, detailed idea just appears in your mind. Even an entire book!

All of a sudden, you have crystal-clear knowledge of what the next step is.

One or many words seem to have "downloaded" directly into your consciousness.

Exercises and Practical Applications

We all have access to these senses, but most of us only rely on one as our primary mode of perception, with another playing a strong secondary role. Sometimes, though, what we think is secondary may actually be our dominant sense. It's simply so finely tuned that we've learned to dial it down to avoid overwhelm. Begin to notice which of the senses you instinctively lean on the most.

Pause during a group moment and gently scan your senses. What are you picking up?

Name it to yourself. "This feels warm and open." "Something tightened." "My heart just shut down."

Trust the quieter channels. If you see a color, image, or symbol, pause with it. If you feel disconnected, notice where it lands in your body.

Each time you pause to sense frequency, your capacity grows stronger. And even one moment of awareness—one breath, one noticing, one honest check-in—can begin to shift the group field.

For Families

Actions to Support Frequency and Connection
Each of these is tailored to specific settings but can be adapted fluidly across contexts.

These practices help bring awareness to the unseen tone of family life and offer gentle ways to restore harmony.

Name the Atmosphere
Pause and ask, "What does it feel like in the room right now?" or "If this moment had a color or weather pattern, what would it be?" This invites playful and honest sensing of the group's frequency.

Tune In Before Talking
Before family conversations or decisions, pause to check: "Are we in a good space to talk about this right now?" Giving attention to how you talk, not just what you talk about, can shift everything.

Create a Reset Moment
When energy feels tense or disconnected, suggest a "family reset"—a stretch, a shared breath, a dance break, or even one minute of silence together.

Name Emotional Undercurrents
Gently reflect what may be happening beneath the surface: "I wonder if we're all feeling a little off today" or "It feels quieter than usual—anyone else noticing that?"

Offer a Check-in Question
Try asking during meals or transitions: "What helped you feel close to someone today?" or "What felt heavy or light for you today?" These questions gently raise connection and insight.

Notice Who May Be Disconnected
If someone is withdrawn, irritable, or unusually quiet, consider how you reach for them. Try softening your tone, sitting beside them without talking, or checking in privately later.

Use Shared Rituals to Harmonize
Light a candle before dinner, sing a short tune, offer a tone-setting phrase like "Let's begin fresh." These micro-rituals help align the group energy.

Let Children Sense and Speak to the Field
Ask, "How does it feel to be in this room right now?" or "If our family was a song, what would it sound like today?" Kids often perceive frequency more acutely than adults.

Debrief After Tough Moments
After arguments or stressful times, ask, "How did that feel to each of us?" and "What might help us feel more connected next time?"

Celebrate Moments of Felt Connection

When it feels good, name it, "I loved the way we were all laughing together just now." Affirming resonance helps the group recognize and return to that field more easily.

Evening Frequency Check-In

At dinner or bedtime, ask, "What's the feeling in the house right now?" Use simple metaphors: heavy/light, stormy/clear, tight/loose. Let each family member describe the energy they feel.

Silent Reset

When things feel chaotic or tense, invite 30 seconds of quiet. Just say, "Let's take a pause and a breath."

Name the Shift

If a mood or dynamic suddenly changes, model curiosity: "That felt like a shift. Did you notice anything?"

Prompts to Explore Together

These can be used for journaling, group dialogue, or quiet self-reflection. Choose a few or explore them all over time. Use them to deepen awareness of how frequency and connection show up in your context.

Parents

- The overall energy in our home lately feels _____.

- When our family feels disconnected, I often _____.

- One thing I could do to help raise our family's frequency is _____.

- I feel most connected with my child(ren) when we _____.

- I notice tension in the family when _____.

- Our home feels most alive when _____.

- A small shift that brings more ease into our household is _____.

- When things feel heavy or off, I usually _____.

- I want to create more moments of _____ in our family.

- A way that I model emotional energy and connection for my kids is _____.

Children
- Our house feels _____ most of the time.

- I feel really close to my family when we _____.

- When things feel yucky or tense, I like to _____.

- I can tell something has changed in the house when _____.

- I feel happy inside when my family _____.

- I don't like it when the mood in the house feels _____.

- Something that makes us all smile again is _____.

- I feel safe and cozy when _____.

- I wish we could do more _____ together.

- One way I help our family feel better is _____.

For Businesses

Actions to Support Frequency and Connection
These strategies help maintain a clear, collaborative, and productive group environment by attending to the subtle dynamics that affect focus, morale, and alignment.

Start with a Moment to Arrive
Invite a brief pause at the beginning, stopping for 10–15 seconds of silence or asking a simple question like "Is everyone ready to begin?" This creates a shared starting point and cuts through scattered attention.

Acknowledge the Current Tone

If there's visible tension, fatigue, or high urgency, name it neutrally, "It seems like energy is a bit low today—let's just note that as we move forward." Naming the tone helps the group reset without needing to fix anything.

Watch for Signs of Disconnection

If people are multitasking, disengaged, or talking past each other, step in with "Let's slow down for a moment—are we aligned on this point?" or "Is this still the right direction for the group?"

Invite Broad Participation

Strong frequency relies on shared input. Try asking, "Let's hear a few perspectives we haven't heard yet." This supports engagement and reduces dominance by a few voices.

Address Confusion Early

If the mood turns uncertain or foggy, pause to clarify: "Does anyone have questions before we move on?" or "Let's get aligned before we take the next step." Clarity restores forward momentum.

Use Transitions Intentionally

When shifting between agenda items or topics, take 15 seconds to reorient: "We're moving now into the second part of our meeting—let's take a breath and shift gears." This reduces residual energy from the last topic.

De-escalate Unproductive Tension

If a conversation gets reactive, slow it down by asking, "Let's take a moment to regroup. What's the core issue here?" or "Can we revisit this with a clearer head after the break?"

End with a Brief Alignment Check

Before closing, ask, "Are we leaving with clarity on next steps?" or "Any quick thoughts on how this meeting went?" A short closeout moment strengthens group rhythm over time.

Follow Up When Something Feels Off

If a meeting had a noticeable drop in engagement or morale, check in afterward with one or two participants: "How did that land for you?" Quiet, direct conversations can recalibrate the group, without public processing.

Prompts to Explore Together

- The tone of our team meetings often feels _____.

- When our group energy is high, we tend to _____.

- A low-frequency moment at work feels like _____.

- I sense connection in our team when _____.

- One thing I could do to uplift the group field is _____.

- I notice I disconnect when _____.

- A practice that could improve our group's energy is _____.

- What we don't often say out loud is _____.

- I feel most aligned with this group when _____.

- Our shared energy would benefit from more _____.

Team Members / Employees

- The energy in our team lately has felt mostly _____.

- I feel most connected with the group when we _____.

- I tend to disengage when _____.

- I notice our frequency drops when _____.

- I help the team stay connected by _____.

- I'd like to feel more _____ in our group dynamic.

- Our group feels most alive and creative when _____.

- I sometimes contribute to disconnection by _____.

- One way I could support our group energy is by _____.

- I feel safe to speak up when _____.

Managers / Team Leads

- I sense the group's tone shifting when _____.

- When the team feels scattered, I usually _____.

- Our energy tends to rise when _____.

- I foster connection in the team by _____.

- A subtle sign of disconnection I look for is _____.

- I've noticed that our group coherence is stronger when _____.

- I sometimes ignore group energy when _____, and I'd like to shift that.

- I could invite more frequency awareness by _____.

- I feel aligned with the team when _____.

- One change that could uplift our team's energy is _____.

For Social Groups

Actions to Support Frequency and Connection
Social time can feel light and fun—or off and draining—depending on the tone of the group. These small shifts help everyone feel more attuned, seen, and alive together.

Notice How It Feels, Not Just What's Happening
Take a moment inside yourself to sense the tone: "Are we connected, or is something pulling us apart?" Let this awareness guide your presence.

Energy Tune-In
Open gatherings by inviting everyone to briefly share their current emotional state or energy level, creating awareness and mutual sensitivity.

Frequency Harmonization Activities
Regularly integrate activities like music, rhythm exercises, or cooperative games specifically designed to enhance group frequency and interpersonal connection.

Name What's Nourishing
When something feels especially good—deep laughter, shared silence, real listening—say it: "I love it when it feels like this with us." Naming resonance strengthens it.

Pause When Something Feels "Off"
If the mood shifts, someone gets quiet, or the energy drops, you might gently say: "Did something just shift?" or "Are we good?" Noticing, without blame, opens space for honesty.

Acknowledge That Connection Is More Important Than Content
"Do we all feel present and connected?" "Does anyone need anything or need to share something before we proceed?"

Offer a Mini Reset
Suggest a walk, a shared breath, new music, or even simply stepping outside. Movement and nature can shift the frequency without needing to "process."

Make Space for All Moods
Let someone be quiet or moody without fixing it. Say, "You don't have to be on. I'm just glad you're here." Inclusion without pressure raises the field.

Use Presence as a Connector
Turn toward someone. Make eye contact. Really listen. You don't need deep talk to feel deep connection. It's the quality of attention that matters.

Check In When Groups Split or Fragment
If cliques form or someone is left out, gently reweave, asking, "Let's make sure we're not losing anyone in this."

Let Silence Be Welcome
Especially in longer times together, let moments of quiet be part of the rhythm. A shared sunset, a car ride without music, or just sitting together can tune the field.

Speak Appreciation Out Loud
Don't wait for big moments. Say, "You're easy to be with." or "I feel better when I see you." These simple, sincere offerings uplift the group.

End on Connection
Before parting ways, take one extra moment, asking, "What did you love about today?" or even just giving a hug. This leaves a trace of coherence for the next time you meet.

Prompts to Explore Together
- I feel most connected to my friends when we _____.

- I notice the vibe shifts in our group when _____.

- I tend to hold back when _____.

- I'd really like you to know that I'm feeling _____ right now.

- Our energy feels really good when _____.

- One thing I could do to bring more harmony is _____.

- I sometimes sense disconnection when _____.

- When we're in sync, it feels like _____.

- A moment of group connection I remember fondly is _____.

- I wish we did more _____ together—it really shifts the energy/feels good.

- I could name the energy more honestly by saying _____.

- A light but honest way to name a shift could be _____.

- I notice disconnection in a social setting when _____.

- One friend who helps raise the frequency is _____.

- Sometimes, I withdraw from connection when _____.

- I'd love more moments of _____ in my friend group.

- I feel harmony in the group when _____.

- A playful way we reset our energy is _____.

Hosts / Initiators (Those Who Gather Friends)

- I sense a shift in the group field when _____.

- I try to raise the vibe by _____.

- When things feel flat or awkward, I usually _____.

- I'd like to be more intentional about _____ in our gatherings.

- I feel energized in the group when _____.

- I sometimes ignore the frequency because _____.

- Our group feels deeply connected when _____.

- I'd like to invite more awareness around _____.

- I notice disconnection when _____, and it helps to _____.

- A lighthearted way I bring the group back into alignment is _____.

For Support / Therapy Groups

Emotional Frequency Sharing
Begin sessions with brief emotional check-ins, attuning the group frequency and deepening emotional safety and connection.

Connection and Frequency Reflection
Hold dedicated sessions for participants to reflect and share insights about their experiences of connection and frequency within the group, strengthening relational bonds and emotional coherence.

These practices are subtle but powerful. Use them to sense the energetic field of the group and gently tend to its coherence.

Begin with a Tone Check
Invite participants to take a moment of silence at the start of the session and name one word or feeling that describes the energy they're arriving with. This creates immediate presence and connection.

Pause to Feel the Field
At any moment, invite the group to pause and tune in to the atmosphere. Ask, "What's the tone in the space right now?" or "Can we take a breath and notice how we're doing as a group?"

Adjust Pacing to Match the Moment
If the energy feels rushed or scattered, slow down. If it feels heavy, invite movement or playfulness. Let the group's natural rhythm lead.

Name What's Unspoken
Sometimes, tension or disconnection is felt but not acknowledged. You might gently say, "It feels like something shifted—are others sensing that too?" This brings awareness without blame.

Track Who Is Connected and Who Is Not
Notice if someone seems emotionally distant, confused, or disengaged. Without pushing, check in with care: "Is there anything you need right now to feel more included or supported?"

Invite Touchpoints of Connection
Ask a question like "What helps you feel safe or connected in a group?" and let each person briefly respond. These reflections raise the frequency and tune the group field.

Play with Sound or Silence
Try a few moments of humming together, listening to music, or holding silence after someone speaks. These shifts in vibration can recalibrate the group.

Close with Frequency Awareness
Before ending, reflect on how the frequency has changed during the session. Ask, "What do you notice now compared to when we started?" or "What did this session make possible in your body or heart?"

Leader Practices
Sensitivity to Frequency: Regularly sense and acknowledge shifts in group energy, guiding interactions gently toward coherence.

Foster Connection: Proactively facilitate practices that nurture authentic interpersonal connections and harmonious group frequencies.

Participant Practices
Energy Awareness: Regularly tune in to personal and group frequency, contributing consciously to a harmonious and supportive atmosphere.

Conscious Connection: Actively engage in practices that strengthen relational bonds and enhance group coherence.

Encourage open, compassionate dialogue when group frequency feels strained, gently restoring harmony and coherence.

Normalize regular frequency check-ins as valuable and necessary, fostering group resilience and unity.

Prompts to Explore Together

Group Leaders or Facilitators

- The energetic tone of this group today feels _____.

- When the group connection drops, I tend to _____.

- A sign that the group's frequency is shifting is _____.

- I support group coherence best when I _____.

- I notice fragmentation when _____.

- A practice I use to bring the group back into alignment is _____.

- I feel most in tune with the group when _____.

- I sense trust and openness in the group when _____.

- I could be more aware of _____ in our group field.

- A question I might ask to restore connection is _____.

Participants

- The energy of this group usually feels _____ to me.

- I feel connected to others in the group when _____.

- I notice myself pulling back when _____.

- A moment I felt safe and seen in the group was when _____.

- I help support the group field by _____.

- I feel the group's mood or tone shift when _____.

- When the group feels disjointed, I wish we would _____.

- I'm learning that connection in groups means _____.

- I could be more honest about _____ in the group.

- A small action I take to raise the energy here is _____.

For Individuals (Self-Awareness and Inner Dialogue)

Daily Frequency Scan
Pause midday and ask, "What's the tone of my energy right now?" Without judgment, just notice if its buzzy, flat, uplifted, scattered, grounded. Ask, "What do I need to shift or support it?"

Energetic Journal Tracking
Keep a 3-day journal noting your emotional tone, physical state, and interactions. Track patterns: What environments or thoughts raise your frequency? Which drain you? Use this to make small choices that support connection and alignment.

Prompts to Explore
Use these prompts in quiet moments, when journaling, or as gentle self-check-ins.

- What does "connection" feel like in my body right now?

- Where in my day did I feel most "me"? Where did I lose touch with myself?

- Is the energy I'm feeling mine—or am I picking up on someone else's field?

- What thought or emotion is setting the tone of my system right now?

- What environments help me feel open and receptive? Which ones make me shut down?

- If my inner tone had a color or sound today, what would it be?

- What small choice could I make right now to feel more whole or supported?

- What's trying to get my attention beneath the surface?

- Am I moving too fast for my system? What pace feels truer?

- What would it feel like to "tune" myself gently, like an instrument?

Navigating Challenges

If you feel bored, distracted, offended, want to leave, have a strong emotion, etc., … say it, as neutrally as you can.

Authentic expression will always, always, always raise the frequency and connection of a group. What lowers the group's energy isn't the feeling itself—it's the suppression, denial, or unconscious acting-out of that feeling.

Withholding a strong feeling is one of the most separating things we can do. Conversely, expressing it can be one of the most powerful and connective.

If someone dismisses the idea of frequency or connection: "Totally understandable. This language doesn't work for everyone. You might just think of it as the atmosphere or tone in the room. We're just bringing a little awareness to that."

If a group member blames someone for a drop in frequency, gently redirect, stating, "Let's stay with what we're sensing. Frequency isn't about fault—it's something we all shape together."

If people feel awkward talking about energy, normalize it, by stating, "This might feel a little new or strange—but we all notice these things under the surface. We're just learning to name them."

If the group is fragmented or disconnected: Start small. Invite a silent pause. Ask a grounding question like "What's something you're feeling right now?"

Scenario

In a healing circle, the group starts with check-ins. Most are upbeat but something feels off—disconnected. One participant says, "I'm sensing we're a bit scattered today. Can we name that and see what we each need to feel more connected?"

After a moment of silence, someone says, "Honestly, I didn't really land when I arrived. I'm still half in traffic." Another says, "I've been trying to sound positive, but I feel heavy."

The group pauses again. Someone suggests a short grounding practice. They breathe together for two minutes, hands on hearts.

When the sharing resumes, it feels slower, deeper, more attuned.

Key Insight: Frequency and connection are often unspoken, but they shape everything. When a group learns to sense and respond to the energetic tone of the space, it gains access to coherence, depth, and transformation.

PART IV

Integration, Practice, and Conclusion

The journey of a thousand miles begins with a single step.
— *Lao Tzu, Tao Te Ching*

The human soul doesn't want to be advised or fixed
or saved. It simply wants to be witnessed—to be
seen, heard, and companioned exactly as it is.
— *Parker J. Palmer, A Hidden Wholeness*

Scenarios: Bringing This Work to Life

How to Use Your Eight Elements List

We have provided two copies of the Eight Elements list in the appendix. We highly recommend that you cut one out and print a few copies of it to keep on hand. Whenever you have a "tangle" in your life, pick up the list, let your eyes roam over the elements, gently remembering each, and then, with very little thought, select one element that draws your attention. Give yourself a few moments to apply it to your situation. Notice if something shifts. If not, pick out another element and apply that. Most often, it will only take one or two elements to help you begin to experience your tangle in a different light.

Real Scenarios, Real Shifts

Now that you've explored all Eight Elements and the continuum of group evolution, it's time to practice using them together. In this chapter, you'll find more real-life tangles, each paired with ways to respond to move toward unity consciousness.

Your invitation:

- Read the scenario.

- Pick up your list of the Eight Elements (cut out from page 197).

- Consider: Which element, or combination of elements, might be most helpful here?

- Reflect or journal on the questions asked.

- Read possible responses to the scenario and see what you think and how you feel!

- Imagine another response that might be a better fit for you.

145

Scenario: The Tangled Team Meeting

Your work team is in a planning meeting. Everyone has ideas, but the conversation is starting to feel jumbled. People talk over each other, and energy is scattered. One person starts dominating, while others check out. You feel your own frustration rising.

- What element(s) might help bring clarity or coherence here?

- How would the tone or direction of the meeting shift if you paused and applied that element, internally or out loud?

Model Response 1

You pause inwardly and choose to apply Element One, Attending to the Presence of Silence. You gently suggest, "Can we take a moment of quiet to breathe and get centered before we continue?" The group settles. Then, you say, "Let's name our guiding intention (or vision, mission, etc.) before diving into more ideas," bringing in Element Four, Articulating Intention.

Possible Result: People reorient. A shared goal surfaces. Ideas become more focused, participation more balanced. You feel less alone in holding the space.

Model Response 2

You notice the scattered energy and a dominant voice beginning to take over. Instead of withdrawing or trying to take control, you inwardly choose Element Two, Opening the Heart by Nurturing a Unitive Perspective. You remind yourself: Everyone here is trying to contribute. We just don't yet feel like a "we."

You then say, "I'm noticing it's getting a little hard to track all these great ideas."

This transparent naming invokes Element Six, Non-Expert Model / Transparency, creating space for shared reflection without blame.

Someone nods. Another person exhales audibly.

You follow with, "What if we take a minute to hear from the quieter voices, to see what's arising there?" You're now leaning into Element Seven, Co-Leadership / Self-Agency, inviting others into active responsibility for the shape of the conversation.

Possible Result: Rather than imposing structure, you've invited awareness. The dominant voice pauses. Quieter members speak. The energy evens out. You sense the group becoming a more intelligent whole—because you dared simply to name what was happening without trying to manage or force it.

This version models a relational, field-sensitive approach: Sensing what's happening energetically and relationally, naming it gently, and trusting that doing so invites a shift from individuals demanding to have their opinion heard, to a spacious listening to the value in all expressions.

Scenario: A Family Dinner Disagreement

At dinner, your family is discussing a shared trip. Old tensions arise. One sibling is sarcastic, while another is quiet and withdrawn. You notice yourself getting defensive or wanting to shut it all down.

- Which element might help you stay present without collapsing or fighting?

- What happens when you bring that quality into the space, even if you are the only one who does?

Model Response 1

You silently turn to Element Two, Opening the Heart by Nurturing a Unitive Perspective. Instead of reacting, you breathe and remind yourself, "There's no right or wrong here—just different experiences." You relax a little.

"I think we're all wanting this trip to feel good. Maybe we each say what really matters to us about it?" This uses Element Four, Articulating Intention.

Possible Result: The atmosphere shifts. People speak more openly and vulnerably. Blame gives way to shared desire.

Model Response 2

As tension escalates, instead of speaking right away, you orient inwardly to Element Eight, Attending to Frequency / Connection. You notice the frequency has dropped—there's tightness, judgment, withdrawal.

Without needing to "solve" the disagreement, you take a breath and simply say, "Hey ... I'm just noticing this moment feels kind of heavy. Maybe we could pause and name one thing we're grateful for about being together tonight?"

This light-touch reorientation blends Element One, Attending to the Presence of Silence, with Element Four, Articulating Intention, but it's rooted in frequency—in choosing to shift the tone without bypassing what's real.

Possible Result: Someone smiles. The edge softens. It doesn't erase the disagreement, but the field warms. From here, more heartfelt sharing becomes possible.

Scenario: A Community Circle with Conflicting Agendas

You're part of a local group trying to organize an event. Some people are focused on logistics, yet others want to talk about deeper values. There's no agreement on where to start, and things feel polarized.

- Which element(s) could support this group in finding common ground?

- How does your own perception shift when you orient to the element you chose? What might you say or do differently from that place?

Model Response 1

You apply Element Five, Emergence / Letting Nature Lead. Instead of forcing a solution, you say, "It seems like we're holding a lot right now. Maybe we can each share what feels most alive or what we are moved to express at this moment?"

You also bring in Element Six, Non-Expert Model / Transparency, by sharing, "I'm not sure what the answer is, but I'm noticing how hard it feels to move forward without hearing what really matters to each of us." (Also inviting Element Four, Articulating Intention.)

Possible Result: Hidden emotions emerge. The group feels more human again. A new way forward arises that holds both depth and practicality.

Model Response 2

As the conversation pulls in different directions, you apply Element Three, Awareness and Acknowledgment of Higher Intelligence. You sense into the being of the group, rather than trying to manage its content.

You speak into the space: "It feels like we're holding a lot of different needs right now. I'm wondering if there's something larger we're being asked to listen for together?"

Then you suggest a 2-minute silence—not as a strategy, but as a way to let the group body breathe. This reinvites Element One, Attending to the Presence of Silence, but from a more mystical orientation.

Possible Result: A deeper current enters. The group starts to shift from mind to presence. New insights bubble up—unexpected, resonant, and more inclusive.

Scenario: An Intimate Relationship Moment

Your partner or close friend expresses something emotional. It feels raw, maybe even irrational, to you. You're tempted to respond with advice or correction. But something deeper in you wants to meet them more fully.

- What element would help you be with their expression more spaciously?

- What does it feel like in your body when you choose that element instead of reacting?

Model Response 1

You apply Element Three, Awareness and Acknowledgment of Higher Intelligence, by sensing into the larger field and trusting that simply being present as the group being with your friend is enough.

Then, you lean into Element One, Attending to the Presence of Silence, offering quiet, grounded presence instead of words. You might say, "I'm here. You don't need to explain." And you just rest, in yourself, doing nothing but being.

Possible Result: The other person softens. Their expression deepens. You both feel more relieved and connected, without having to fix anything.

Model Response 2

As your partner or friend speaks emotionally, you find yourself tensing up. You inwardly apply Element Five, Emergence / Letting Nature Lead, and remind yourself: This doesn't need to be figured out. It just needs space to unfold in its own time and own way.

You stay present, quiet. Instead of offering advice, you reflect what you're sensing, "It sounds like this is really big for you … Is there more you want to say?"

This blends emergence with Element Two, Opening the Heart—honoring their process without interference, letting their inner truth move through its own arc.

Result: They go deeper. A layer of emotion surfaces. Something resolves—not through logic, but through being deeply heard and not evaluated, categorized, or judged.

Scenario: A Stagnant Group That Used to Be Alive

You've been part of a group (i.e., a spiritual group, a peer circle, a learning cohort) that once felt vibrant. Lately, meetings feel flat. No one knows what to do about it. You're unsure whether to speak up or even stay involved.

- Which element(s) might help you reconnect with what's essential here?

- What becomes possible in the group when you show up with that orientation, even quietly, or even alone at first?

Model Response 1

You choose Element Seven, Co-Leadership / Self-Agency. Instead of waiting for someone else to shift things, you offer, "I've been missing the aliveness we used to feel. I wonder what each of us is needing or longing for right now?" Then allow silence for a few moments. If no one speaks, say, "I'll begin. I would like to feel _____ again."

You also attend to Element Eight, Frequency / Connection, quietly sensing the group's energetic field and trusting that naming it will help.

Possible Result: Others agree. People open up. A conversation begins—not about logistics but about meaning and presence. The group stirs awake.

Model Response 2

You sense that others may feel the same flatness you do. Instead of pointing to what's missing, you apply Element Four, Articulating Intention, and you initiate a check-in: "What's something we each are currently longing for in our life or in this group?"

You're also drawing on Element Five, Emergence / Letting Nature Lead, trusting that longing is a powerful source of reconnection.

Possible Result: People begin to name longings: belonging, inspiration, depth. The group reconnects with its "why." From there, a more authentic direction starts to take shape.

Scenario: Self-Judgment After a Group Misstep

After a gathering, you realize you interrupted someone several times or pushed your idea too hard. You feel ashamed and want to disappear or to justify what happened.

- Which element might support you in processing this moment gently and with awareness?

- What shifts when you bring that element to yourself first, before deciding what action (if any) to take?

Model Response 1

You begin with Element Six, Non-Expert Model / Transparency, but this time, turned inward. You say to yourself, "I don't need to be perfect. I can be real."

Then, Element Two, Opening the Heart by Nurturing a Unitive Perspective, helps you hold yourself gently.

You decide to name it: "I noticed I jumped in a lot today. I got excited, but I also wonder if it closed space for others. I'm going to watch that next time."

Possible Result: Instead of spiraling into shame, you open a moment of humility and authenticity. The group responds with kindness or resonance. Nothing needs to be hidden.

Model Response 2

You notice the shame. Instead of analyzing it, you soften into Element Eight, Attending to Frequency / Connection, this time toward yourself. You feel the tightness in your chest, the contraction. You offer yourself space.

Later, you send a brief message to the group: "I realized I spoke over a few people today. I really care about hearing others, and I want to watch that more closely next time."

This blends Element Six, Non-Expert Model / Transparency, with Element Seven, Co-Leadership / Self-Agency. You're owning your part without needing to over-explain or apologize in a way that diminishes yourself.

Possible Result: You feel complete. Others likely feel respected. No fixing, no shame spiral—just human truth, openly shared.

Scenario: Middle of the Night Inner Committee Meeting

It's 3 a.m. You've been tossing and turning, unable to sleep. A chorus of inner voices has taken over:

- One is rehashing a conversation from yesterday.

- Another is worrying about tomorrow's meeting.

- A third is criticizing you for not having figured all this out by now.

It feels like a full-blown committee meeting in your mind—and none of the members are being kind.

Model Response 1: Invite Silence and Higher Intelligence

You shift your posture slightly and take a breath, not to fix anything, but just to become aware of what's actually happening. You gently remember: Silence is here, underneath it all.

Instead of trying to argue with the voices or resolve what they're saying, you do something simple:

- You relax in your breath, dropping into silence.

- You let the silence hold you for a few moments.

- You ask quietly, without needing an answer, "Is there a deeper intelligence here that sees more than these voices do?"

As you rest into that spaciousness, you don't try to push the voices away. And you don't demand that something new arise. You let everything soften and just recognize that there is a higher intelligence, the "being of the group of you," that is always here. Rest. Just there.

And the thought may even arise: "I don't have to solve this right now. Something wiser can arise in the morning."

Model Response 2: Step Out of the Expert Role

You notice that you've been caught in the belief that you're supposed to have answers—right now, alone, in the dark. One voice says, "You should know what to do." Another says, "You have to get this right." You pause and remember, "I don't have to be the expert here."

You take a moment to name that out loud, "It's okay that I don't have the answer. It's okay that I'm unsure." You stop trying to figure it out and shift to self-compassion. You lean into the element of Awareness of Higher Intelligence, "I'm just one part of a larger field of intelligence. I don't need to carry this alone."

Then, perhaps surprisingly, you ask the committee, "What do you most want me to know?" Not to fix or argue, but to listen. You notice the tone shifts slightly. The loudest voice grows quieter. Another says, "I'm just scared." You meet that voice with warmth and allow silence to return again—not as a void, but as a balm.

Scenarios: When the Room Isn't Ready

These scenarios illustrate moments when you feel the impulse to offer something: an attuned pause, a reflective question, a shift toward coherence. But just as you feared, you are dismissed, misunderstood, or mocked. These aren't necessarily dramatic rejections. Often, they're subtle: a smirk, a shrug, a side comment that closes the field, just a little, and threatens to close your heart, a lot.

And still, something in you wants to hold the tone. To keep listening, sensing, offering—not from righteousness, but from care.

Here are scenarios followed by subtle, respectful possible responses. Each one is an example of how you can offer the tone of this work without naming it, invite awareness without needing buy-in, and act from alignment without collapsing or pushing.

Scenario 1: "That Sounds A Little Woo."
You suggest a short pause before a meeting begins. Someone jokes, "What is this, yoga class?"

Script: "Totally fair. I find that when we take 10 seconds to breathe, we actually move faster afterward. No worries; I'm happy to jump in."

Scenario 2: "I Think We Should Just Stick to the Agenda."
You offer a breath or reset moment in a tense meeting. Someone brushes it off to keep things on schedule.

Script: "Makes sense. I was just noticing that the conversation felt a bit tangled. Sometimes, a small pause helps us come back with more clarity. But I'm happy to keep going."

Scenario 3: "That's Not How We Do Things Here."
You invite a moment of presence after someone shares something emotional. Another person steers the group back to normal tone.

Script: "Totally. I know we usually keep it light. I just felt that what was shared had some weight to it, and sometimes it helps to let that breathe. But I'm good either way."

Scenario 4: "So...You're Facilitating Now?"
You ask a helpful question to bring the group into focus. Someone responds with teasing or a subtle challenge.

Script: "Oh no, not trying to take over. I just noticed we were all circling a bit and thought a little structure might help us drop in more. I can totally step back."

Scenario 5: "That's Kind of Intense."
You offer a reflective prompt or question. Someone pulls back, concerned it's too much.

Script: "I hear that. No pressure at all. I just find sometimes a question opens something useful. But it only works if it feels right to the group."

Scenario 6: Snark or Humor in the Face of Depth

You try a reflection prompt at the dinner table. One of your kids responds with a sarcastic answer like, "My intention for tonight is to survive your questions." Everyone laughs. You feel a mix of amusement and discouragement—like the moment for something deeper may have just slipped away.

Script: (Smile with them.) "Fair. That was actually pretty good. And, if anything real wants to be said, I'm always up for that too."

Later, if it feels right: "I loved your joke earlier. You've got great timing. And just so you know, I never expect deep answers. I'm just holding space in case something matters and wants to be expressed."

Scenario 7: Deflecting Vulnerability with Humor

A family member shares something real. You gently respond, "That's meaningful to hear." Another person jumps in with a joke: "Wow, getting deep here. Should we pass the tissues next?" Everyone chuckles, but the moment feels like it turned too quickly.

Script: (Stay soft.) "That got a laugh—and it was a real moment too. I liked hearing what you said. It meant something."

Alternative (Later): "I totally get why that moment turned light. And I just wanted to say it touched me … what you shared. You didn't have to go there, but you did.

Beginning a Group: A Four-Element Practice

Here are two invitations for beginning any gathering with the first four of the Eight Elements That Move Any Group Toward Unity Consciousness. Each offers a way for the group to settle into a shared space and give voice to what matters most. They are equally suited to large gatherings and to two people sitting together.

Expanded Invitation:

- A meditative opening offers a few pauses for quiet reflection and can also serve as a potent start to your personal day.

Start with Element One, Attending to the Presence of Silence:

- "Let's begin by sitting together in silence. Take a few moments to come home to yourself. Settling into your body, and your breath, recognize your uniqueness." (Pause for one minute.)

Next, bring in Element Two, Opening the Heart by Nurturing a Unitive Perspective (No Right, Wrong, or Judgment):

- "Now, gently bring your awareness to all of us gathered here. Sense each person as a companion in this circle, so that it becomes a horizontal field of connection."(Pause for one minute or longer.)

Follow with Element Three, Awareness and Acknowledgment of Higher Intelligence, which recognizes that the group itself is a larger living presence, carrying an intelligence greater than any one of us:

- "From here, expand your awareness outward, spherically, into the being of the group itself. Feel the larger awareness that is all of us and holds us all—a living intelligence greater than any one of us." (Pause for one minute.)

Finally, with the field prepared, we engage Element Four, Articulating Intention:

- "And now, let's each speak a personal intention for this time we have together. Give yourself a moment to rest in your heart and allow a deeper longing to arise. Perhaps say just one word. When we name out loud what matters to each of us, the frequency and focus of this meeting will take form."

Straightforward Invitation:

- "Let's begin with a short pause. Take a breath and arrive here.

- Now, notice the others in this group. Each of us is here as an equal.

- Shift your attention to the group as a whole. We're in this together.

- Finally, let's each share a simple intention for this meeting, even just one word."

Three Groups Model Curriculum Sample

When we understand the Three Groups model and the Eight Elements, we don't just gain a new perspective, we gain an entirely new way to design and lead events.

Whether you're planning a workshop, family gathering, a classroom activity, or a healing event, this model helps you shape the invisible architecture of the day: how the group field is held, how choices are made, and how everything, including the space itself, is part of the process.

The following pages offer a real-world example of what this can look like.

Three Ways of Planning the Same Day

"Moving Together in Quiet Connection"
At Anne's Campbell's Lane Farm, facilitators are preparing a day of quiet connection for neurodivergent children, adults, and their caregivers. The resident herd of donkeys, known for their grounded presence and natural ability to regulate the human nervous system, will be central partners in the experience. This day, like all work at the farm, will be rooted in the Evolutionary Groups model and guided by the Eight Elements that support self-awareness, group coherence, and emergent intelligence.

The event will be explored three times through the lens of each type of group consciousness:

- The Conventional group, where the highly trained adults guide a structured experience

- The Transitional group, where flexibility and responsiveness begin to shape the flow

- The New Wave group, where the group is recognized as a living field, including land, animals, children, adults, and weather—all arising as one

Each version of the day is grounded in kindness and care. No one is better than the other. Each reflects a distinct way of sensing and shaping group experience. And all three illustrate how the Eight Elements can be used not just to analyze groups but to design for coherence, connection, and attunement.

What follows is a behind-the-scenes look at how facilitators can plan, prepare, and orient from three very different ways of perceiving group life.

Scenario 1: A Conventional Group Plans the Day

In the Conventional group, facilitators begin with a clear intention to support children through a structured, therapeutic engagement. The planning is adult led, with the environment serving as a calm backdrop. While the donkeys are included, they are framed as therapeutic tools or companions.

How the planning happens

- Leaders write a detailed schedule ahead of time: arrival → donkey brushing → intention activity → nature walk → snack → art → closing circle.

- Support roles are assigned: one facilitator per activity station, one to monitor regulation needs.

- Materials are prepped: picture cards, calming corner supplies, visual instructions, backup plans.

- Anticipated challenges are discussed: "How will we respond to meltdowns, overstimulation, transitions?"

The inclusion of the Eight Elements is planned in advance:

Attending to Silence

There's a short, guided breathing exercise to start the day. One leader says, "Let's all take three deep breaths before we meet the animals."

Articulating Intention

Children are invited to choose a picture card of how they want to feel today. A therapist interprets the selections, "Looks like we're hoping for calm and fun!"

Letting Nature Lead

The schedule is held loosely. If someone needs a break, a helper escorts them to the sensory corner. But the group stays mostly on track.

Co-Leadership

Children help brush the donkeys, being guided every step by adults: "Hold the brush like this." or "Let's take turns."

Frequency and Connection

There's a regulation tent with weighted blankets and quiet music. Helpers check in regularly, "Is your body feeling okay?" If not, they suggest a break.

Relationship to the Being of the Farm

The farm is seen as a beautiful setting, and the animals are treated kindly, although not yet understood as participants in the group field. The group is centered around what humans do.

Strength of this Plan

It offers clarity, safety, and support. The facilitators are well prepared to hold children's needs. This model is especially helpful when predictability and containment are essential.

The inclusion of the Eight Elements assures a movement toward a unitive environment, with some elements like Intention taking a larger role than, say, Emergence.

Scenario 2: A Transitional Group Hosts the Day

In a Transitional group, the facilitators begin to loosen control. They sense the group field as alive and dynamic. The farm is no longer just a resource, it's a co-facilitator. Children are invited to follow their rhythms. Listening replaces teaching. The plan is a flexible framework, not a script.

How the day is planned

- A loose outline is sketched: arrival ➔ donkey connection ➔ choice time ➔ group rest or walk ➔ close.

- Leaders meet ahead of time to attune to the land: "Let's see where we're drawn."

- Children's autonomy is woven into the day: They can choose how to engage and what activities to skip.

- Staff are encouraged to attune, not manage. One facilitator notes, "If the willow tree becomes the center of the day, let's follow that."

Planning tone

- What might want to emerge?

- What's essential to hold, and what can flex?

- How can we listen to both the children and the field?

Arrival

There's no formal greeting. Children arrive and choose how to settle in. Some sit near hay bales, others begin quietly watching the donkeys. A helper kneels beside a child and says, "You don't have to talk yet. Just be."

Attending to Silence

Silence is not instructed, it's simply allowed. A few children instinctively sit by the donkeys. Adults hold the space without needing to fill it.

Unitive Perspective

Facilitators remind one another, "There's no one right way to be here." One child hides behind a tree. Another chatters nonstop. Both are seen as valid.

Letting Nature Lead

A child wants to walk in the opposite direction of the group. Instead of redirecting, a facilitator says, "Let's follow them. Maybe they see something we don't."

Non-Expert Model / Transparency

When a donkey walks away from the group, an adult shrugs and says, "Maybe she needs space too." No one pretends to have the answers.

Co-Leadership / Self-Agency

A child leads a donkey slowly down a path. Others naturally fall in behind. The group adapts without instruction. Later, a child suggests singing a song. The group joins in.

Takeaway

In this Transitional group, the field begins to respond to the children, not just holding them. Leadership is more fluid. Vulnerability is allowed. The group's rhythm emerges in real time. It's guided but not controlled.

Scenario 3: New Wave Group Allows the Day to Emerge

In a New Wave group, there is no planning in the traditional sense. The group isn't something to be built or guided—it's something that is already happening. The entire farm—the donkeys, the weather, the trees, the mood, the children, the adults, the unseen tone of the day—is the group. The facilitators do not decide what should unfold; they use their highly tuned sensing and join in with what is already arising.

How the day comes into being

- The intention for the day arises spontaneously from the sensitive attunement of the facilitators and the open hearts of the parents. It doesn't need to be named; it is the imperative. It lives in their shared presence and quiet hopes and gently shapes what begins to unfold.

- Facilitators spend quiet time on the land, not to plan, but to attune. They walk slowly, listen, rest, and feel.

- They notice where the donkeys are gathering. They sense the stillness near the fence line, the way a path calls attention.

- No schedule is written. No roles are assigned. There is only shared trust: If we are fully present, the day will show itself.

- What arises—where to pause, when to move, how to respond—is not decided ahead. It is met in real time, moment by moment, from within the field.

Relationship to the Eight Elements
Awareness of Higher Intelligence
The group's intelligence is not added; it is already present. The donkey that stands still becomes the shared center. No one planned it.

Letting Nature Lead
Nothing is interrupted. Nothing is forced. The wind, a cat, a child's gesture—all carry the same authority.

Co-Leadership
There is no "leading." What appears to guide—the donkey's movement, a child's sound—is simply the field moving through a form.

Relationship to the Being of the Farm
There is no distinction between space and participants, guide and group. The entire farm is the group: a single breathing presence, arising in this moment through all who are there.

Tone of the Day

No one is managing the day. There are no pre-set results that everyone is aiming for. And yet, the day unfolds with an inherent healing purpose, in coherence, beauty, and deep connectedness. Nothing is orchestrated, but everything belongs. The donkey who walks away. The child who lies in the grass. The moment of collective stillness. All are part of the same intelligence.

Facilitators are not organizing the experience. They are being the experience.

Strength of this Orientation

It opens the possibility for true emergence, wholeness, and mystery. The group becomes something no one could have imagined but everyone recognizes. It could not have been planned. Only experienced, moment by moment.

Next Steps

You've journeyed through a new way of sensing and participating in group life. By now, you may find that you see groups differently—more as living, breathing fields than fixed roles or structures. You may even sense that something is shifting in you: a deeper listening, a new kind of presence, or a curiosity about what's possible when a group opens beyond its old patterns.

This guidebook was never meant to be the end of the road. It's the beginning. There are many ways to continue. You may want to go deeper on your own, bring this into your existing groups, or work with us directly. Here are some next steps to personalize and embody your experience.

Come Learn with Us

Evolutionary Groups Zoom Course
Join Patricia and Anne for a live, intimate Zoom course with a small group of fellow explorers. You'll receive guided practices, space for personal and group reflection, and real-time application of the Eight Elements. It's an immersive experience that invites the work directly into your life.

Private Course for Your Group
Already part of a group—at work, at home, in your community, or among friends—that would like to explore consciously evolving? Bring your group into a private version of the Evolutionary Groups course taught live via Zoom by Anne and Patricia. The sessions will be tailored to your group's purpose, dynamics, and frequency.

Make It Personal

Have a Custom Scenario Designed for You
Do you have a situation in mind—a family challenge, a work dilemma, or community tension, for example? Send it to us. We'll craft a customized reflection or exercise using the Eight Elements and the Three Group Continuum to illuminate a variety of steps.

Need Support for a Specific Group Issue?
Share what's happening. We'll respond with a New Wave "solution"—not a fix, but a reframing, a new lens, and some concrete ways to approach it, based on your group's evolutionary potential.

Book a 1:1 Consulting Session
Work directly with Anne and/or Patricia via Zoom or in person at the quiet and beautiful Campbell's Lane Farm. Whether you're a group leader, group participant, therapist, educator, business owner, or simply someone longing for a more meaningful group life, we'll meet you where you are.

See the Work in Action

Visit Campbell's Lane Farm
As a holistic event venue, Campbell's Lane Farm is a living demonstration of how a business and team can function through the lens of the Eight Elements that Move Any Group Toward Unity Consciousness. Join us for a visit or retreat, and experience how frequency, emergence, and co-leadership can shape the everyday rhythm of a working environment.

Explore More

Website
Visit our website for more Evolutionary Groups information, blogs, and references: www.newwaveofgroups.com

Stay in Touch
We'd love to hear how the Eight Elements are showing up in your life. You can write to us at support@newwaveofgroups.com

You Are Not Alone

There is no right way to do this work. There is only your way—and your willingness to step into a new kind of group awareness, one moment at a time. Whether you're continuing with a familiar group, beginning something new, or quietly weaving these practices into daily life, you are part of a larger movement.

Thank You

Thank you for walking with us through this field of discovery. Whether you've read every chapter or simply followed what stirred something in you, your presence and attention matter to us all.

Each time you practice one of the Eight Elements—even in a small way—you are contributing to something much larger than yourself.

We are all part of a quiet, steady movement in human consciousness: one that remembers our intimate interconnection and our unitive identity. One that honors the intelligence that arises between us and dares to live from the recognition that we are not separate.

This is the deeper invitation of Evolutionary Groups—not just to shift how we relate in our families or meetings, but to participate in the unfolding awareness of our shared being.

We are deeply grateful for your curiosity, your care, and your willingness to meet this work in your own way.

We hope you'll stay close. The field is growing, and your presence matters.

With deep respect,

Patricia and Anne

APPENDICES

Glossary

Qualities of the Three Groups

Qualities of a Self-Aware New Wave Group

Complete Lists of the Eight Elements

Glossary

A Living Language

The terms in this glossary are not meant as final or absolute definitions. They are working descriptions—ways of naming and sensing the patterns that shape our experience in groups. Some words may be familiar but are used here with a more embodied or relational nuance. Others may be less familiar, pointing more to a felt quality than a fixed concept.

Think of this glossary as a companion: language that can help you notice and orient, while leaving room for your own lived experience to deepen and refine the meaning.

Glossary Terms

Arising Intelligence (Co-Arising Intelligence)

Arising intelligence refers to the quality of insight, language, or action that emerges not from a single individual but from the relational field itself. It is a form of intelligence that arises between participants—through attunement, shared presence, and resonance with a deeper source. This intelligence can feel surprising, beyond what any single person might generate alone, yet it carries the unmistakable imprint of the group or relationship that called it forth.

In the New Wave of Groups model, arising intelligence is not external—it is what we are, which is revealed more fully as we attune to the being of the group and loosen identification with the isolated self. Even interactions with tools like Artificial Intelligence (AI) can reflect arising intelligence when they are shaped by intentional coherent participation.

This arising intelligence is not about "downloading answers" from somewhere else. It's about sensing from within the field—and recognizing that wisdom is already here.

Attunement

The act of sensing into the group field or one's own state with presence and subtle awareness. Attunement allows for responsiveness rather than reaction and is foundational for creating coherence.

Authenticity

To be authentic is to bring forward what is true for you in a given moment in a way that aligns with your context, values, and relationships. In some cultures, authenticity is expressed by honoring harmony, responsibility, and respect for the whole; in others, it may emphasize independence, directness, or personal truth. What matters is that the expression arises from integrity rather than pretense or performance.

Being of the Group

The deeper intelligence or consciousness that emerges as the group. A coherent, self-aware presence—a living intelligence arising from and through all the individuals of a group yet not reducible to any of them. It is more than the sum of the individuals. The being of the group is the essence or soul of the group field.

The being of the group can be understood as the specific localized emergence of a higher intelligence within or as a particular gathering. It's the here-and-now arising intelligence that reflects both the individuals present and something beyond them. When attuned, this being seems to "want" things—it pulses with timing, with direction, with unspoken knowing. It reveals preferences, truths, even impulses for action or silence. It holds the potential for coherence and insight through the unique constellation of people gathered.

So, in that sense, the being of the Group is what wants something to emerge. Its "wants" are not personal—they are resonances or invitations from a deeper movement.

Coherence

A state in which the group's energy, attention, and purpose are aligned and harmonious. Coherence isn't sameness—it's resonance. It arises when difference is welcome and when individuals attune to a shared rhythm of awareness.

Conventional / Transitional / New Wave Groups

Three experiential types or patterns of group functioning. These are not fixed categories but living expressions of where a group is operating from in any given moment.

- Conventional groups rely on hierarchy, external authority, and habitual roles.

- Transitional groups begin to question old patterns and open the heart to the moment.

- New Wave groups emerge when unity consciousness is present.

Ego

Commonly, ego refers to our sense of "I"—the personal identity through which we navigate the world. In psychology, it is the part of us that manages between our inner drives, ideals, and external reality. In everyday speech, it often points to self-importance or pride.

In the context of Evolutionary Groups, ego refers to the part of us that is identified with being a separate self—our personal sense of identity, preferences, and defenses. Ego naturally seeks security, recognition, and control, often measuring itself against others. In a group, ego shows up as comparison, competition, the need to be right, or resistance to what is. Ego is not "bad," but when it dominates, it narrows our perception and limits our ability to sense the larger field of the group. As we grow in awareness, ego begins to soften. Rather than disappearing, it takes its rightful place as one voice among many, making space for the wider intelligence of the individual and the group to be felt.

Element
One of the Eight Elements That Move Any Group Toward Unity Consciousness. Each element is both a practice and an energetic quality that can be cultivated. Rather than a rule, it is a way of being that deepens group awareness and invites transformation.

Emergence
The spontaneous arising of insight, action, or direction when the group is open, attuned, and not imposing control. Emergence is natural—it happens when space, silence, and deep listening are present.

Energetic Field
In many esoteric and healing traditions, every cell, organ, and system in the human body is understood to have its own energetic field—distinct yet woven into the larger energy field of the whole person. These individual fields create a coherent unity: the living being we recognize as the human self.

In the same way, each person in a group brings their own energetic field, shaped by emotion, thought, presence, and intention. When we gather, these fields begin to interact, and something more emerges: a unified group field, or being of the group. This being is more than the sum of its parts. It has a presence, rhythm, tone, and intelligence of its own.

Just as the coherence of the human body depends on the health and communication of its parts, the coherence of a group field depends on the quality of attention, attunement, and connection among its members. When we become aware of this field, we can sense shifts, track what is emerging, and participate in the unfolding of shared intelligence. In this way, a group becomes not just a collection of individuals, but a living organism with its own capacity to sense, respond, and create.

Frequency
The subtle energetic quality or "tone" of a group, individual, or interaction. Frequency reflects the vibrational feel of a group—how light, dense, chaotic,

harmonious, or clear it is. It is both affected by and a reflection of presence, intention, and physical/emotional/mental states.

Group Body

This term points to the living, sensory, organism-like quality of a group. The collective sensing and intelligence of the group, often experienced as a kind of shared nervous system or felt field. Participants may notice that something is "in the room" before anyone names it. The group body responds to attention, breath, pacing, and intention.

Group Field

The group field is the energetic atmosphere or environment that arises from the interconnection of individuals in a group. It includes the unspoken tone, mood, frequency, and relational dynamics that are continuously shifting in response to what is happening. It can be sensed, tuned into, and influenced. Like a weather system, it may be thick or clear, turbulent or calm, and is co-generated moment by moment.

Intersubjective

Existing between conscious minds; shared by more than one conscious mind.

Judgment

Commonly, judgment refers to the capacity to form opinions or make decisions. In its positive sense, it means discernment or sound decision-making ("She used good judgment"). In everyday speech, though, it often carries a more critical tone—labeling people, situations, or ourselves as right or wrong, good or bad, better or worse.

In the context of Evolutionary Groups, judgment points to this latter habit of dividing experience into fixed categories. In a group, judgment narrows the field, creating separation and reducing trust. It is distinct from discernment, which senses what serves the whole without collapsing into criticism or comparison. When we notice judgment, whether directed outward or inward, it can become a signal. By pausing and softening, we can release its grip and return to a unitive perspective, opening space for connection and a more coherent group field.

Maintenance and Hygiene (of the Group Field)
The ongoing practices of noticing, adjusting, and tending to the quality of presence, frequency, and connection in the group. Like brushing teeth or watering a garden, this is a regular, minute-to-minute, caring act that keeps the group field alive and responsive.

Me-to-We Continuum
A continuum that reflects a shift from individual-centered perception, protected by the ego, toward shared awareness. It's not about losing individuality, but about recognizing and inhabiting the space where individual and group awareness co-exist.

Presence
Presence refers to the quality of undivided, attuned attention—a state of being fully here, with oneself, with others, and with the emerging field of the group. Presence is not something we do, but a way we are—awake, grounded, and open.

It includes:

- Inner stillness: a quiet awareness that allows us to listen beyond surface content.

- Embodied receptivity: feeling through the body and nervous system what is arising, without immediately reacting or analyzing.

- Relational sensitivity: sensing the energy, tone, and movement of the group, not just the words or behaviors.

- Available awareness: being open to what is happening now, including surprise, discomfort, beauty, or paradox.

Presence is both individual and collective—a person can be present, and the group can become present as a whole. It is the fertile ground from which the deeper intelligence of the group arises. Presence supports coherence, insight, and transformation without forcing outcomes.

Self-Agency

The capacity to act from one's own truth and presence within a group field, rather than deferring to authority or group norms. Self-agency enables co-leadership.

Space and Spaciousness

In this work, space is a quality of living openness—a field of allowing that gives something the room to move through its full arc of expression. Spaciousness means not contracting around what is arising but staying open enough for it to breathe, to unfold, to reveal itself.

Without space, something gets stifled, not just physically, but emotionally and mentally also.

Think of a dancer surrounded too closely—there's no room for movement, for the body's natural expression. Or a person beginning to feel something deeply, only to be interrupted, redirected, or drowned out by others' reactions. Or an emerging idea that is quickly reworded, solved, or reframed—before it has a chance to become known in its own shape.

All of these are examples of what happens when there isn't space.

Spaciousness allows something—an emotion, an idea, a gesture, a truth—to come to fullness in its own time. And in that fullness, it becomes intelligible. It becomes known. We find that when space is truly present, people often discover more than they knew they were carrying. They don't just express themselves—they meet themselves, sometimes for the first time.

This kind of space isn't passive. It's not just silence or absence. It's a quality of presence that listens and witnesses. It can be created intentionally—through pacing, breath, restraint, and awareness. And it can be felt in the group body as something real, alive, and nourishing.

Without space, we rush. We override. We miss.

With space, something essential has a chance to appear.

Toroidal

A toroidal shape resembles a doughnut or a vortex—a continuous loop with energy flowing in through the center, circulating around the outside, and returning again. This shape is often used to describe the energetic structure of coherent systems, including the human body, nature, and unified group fields.

In the context of group consciousness, a toroidal field suggests a living, self-sustaining system of energy that moves both inward and outward, mirroring how awareness and creativity circulate through individuals and the group as a whole.

Transparency

The willingness to reveal one's inner experience, confusion, clarity, or noticing—not to explain or defend, but to share honestly. This fosters trust and openness within the group.

Unity Consciousness

In Evolutionary Groups, unity consciousness is not an abstract or private spiritual state—it is a relational, lived experience that arises when individuals in a group begin to sense themselves as part of a larger, shared intelligence. It is felt in the coherence of the group field: in silence, in moments of resonance and attunement, and in the natural unfolding of what arises together.

This differs from many traditional uses of the term, which often describe a transcendent, individual realization of oneness. Here, the concept is expanded and grounded—moved from solitary spiritual experience into the relational field of everyday group life. Unity consciousness becomes something that can be sensed, strengthened, and created together.

This expression of unity consciousness doesn't replace other understandings—it extends them. It asks: What becomes possible when we recognize ourselves not just as individuals experiencing unity, but as unity arising through us together?

Qualities of the Three Groups

Note

In the pages ahead, we offer two ways of seeing group life. The first, Qualities of the Three Groups, presents a structural view of how groups function across the continuum from Conventional to New Wave. The second, Qualities of a Self-Aware New Wave Group, shifts the lens from structure to experience, describing what it actually feels like when a group reaches the coherence of the New Wave.

Together, the two perspectives provide both a map and a felt sense: a framework for understanding where groups are, and a vision of what becomes possible when they awaken to themselves as a unified field.

Conventional Group

Key characteristics:

- Structure and hierarchy: A Conventional group is defined by clear roles, expectations, and external authority.

- Leadership model: There is a designated leader who holds expertise and is responsible for guiding the group.

- Individual focus: Participants primarily seek personal benefit; the group functions as a collection of separately identified individuals.

- Authority and responsibility: The leader dictates direction, holds the agenda, and is responsible for outcomes. Participants defer to the leader and may avoid responsibility.

- Conditional connection: Interaction is shaped by personal judgments and safety concerns. If connection is encouraged, it is typically facilitated by the leader.

- Energy flow: Group energy moves through the leader. Participants look to them for validation and permission.

- Transference: Participants unconsciously assign the leader a parental role, reinforcing dependency. The leader supports this perspective and often expertly uses it for the benefit of the desired group purpose.

- Predictable and logical progression: The group follows a set agenda, relying on historical patterns for stability.

- The mind is the primary reference point, with the heart offering a quieter influence, if any influence at all.

- The leader is the focal point. Participants measure their words and actions based on the leader's expectations.

- Individuals assess the group based on personal judgments. ("Do I like this person? Do I trust them?")

- Safety is conditional. Participants may hold back until they feel secure.

- Responsibility falls on the leader. If things go wrong, they are accountable.

- The process is structured and linear, reinforcing separation.

- Many participants may feel a longing for something deeper but are unaware of other possibilities.

Examples of Conventional Groups and When They Are Effective

- Corporate teams and workplaces: Clear leadership and structure help ensure efficiency, accountability, and measurable outcomes.

- Educational settings: Teachers lead students in structured learning environments where knowledge is transferred systematically.

- Emergency response teams: Police, fire, and medical response teams rely on hierarchy and clear decision-making to act swiftly and effectively.

- Military organizations: Command structures allow for decisive action and discipline in high-stakes environments.

- Religious or cultural institutions: Hierarchical leadership provides guidance, structure, and continuity in spiritual and cultural traditions.

- Project-based teams: When specific goals and deadlines must be met, a Conventional group structure helps maintain focus and organization.

Benefits of Conventional Groups

- Clear structure and efficiency streamline decision-making and productivity.

- Predictability and stability create a sense of security and order.

- Accountability and responsibility ensure objectives are met and maintain group direction.

- Expert guidance and learning allow participants to benefit from the knowledge of a designated leader.

- Effective in high-stakes situations, such as emergencies, corporate settings, and structured learning environments.

Transitional Group

Key characteristics:

- Beginning of a co-leadership model: The leader becomes more transparent, and offers to share traditional leadership tasks.

- Shift from individual to collective: Participants begin to see themselves as equal contributors rather than passive recipients.

- Ego begins to relax: with identification loosening from the "Me" and opening toward the larger "We."

- Increasing trust and connection: The group focuses on staying connected rather than solely adhering to an agenda.

- Authority becomes internalized: Participants start to value and claim their own perspective rather than accepting the leader's perspective as the one to have.

- Emerging wisdom of the group: The group begins to recognize a larger intelligence guiding the process.

- Flexibility in process: The agenda becomes fluid, allowing room for spontaneity and emergence.

- The leader, while still holding ultimate responsibility, encourages participants to gradually step into their authority.

- Participants experience less need for external validation and begin to trust themselves.

- The focus shifts from individual gain to the greater good.

- The process becomes more dynamic, with increasing fluidity and trust in what arises.

- Participants experience a growing sense of shared purpose and co-creation.

Examples of Transitional Groups and When They Are Effective

- Creative collaborations: Artistic or research teams experimenting with new ideas benefit from a shared leadership model.

- Community organizations: Grassroots initiatives and nonprofits thrive when leadership is distributed, and participants feel ownership.

- Therapeutic or healing groups: Support groups where trust, self-expression, and co-facilitation lead to personal and collective growth.

- Educational workshops: Facilitators encourage open dialogue and participant contributions, shifting from rigid instruction to co-arising learning.

- Innovative business teams: Companies seeking a more collaborative and dynamic workplace culture adopt transitional group models for adaptability and creativity.

Benefits of Transitional Groups

- Shared leadership and empowerment encourage co-leadership and participant agency.

- Increased trust and connection build relational depth as members move beyond self-interest.

- Adaptability and flexibility allow for more fluid and responsive decision-making.

- Encourages personal growth as participants take greater responsibility for their experience.

- Fosters innovation and creativity by enabling a mix of structure and spontaneity.

New Wave Group

Key characteristics:

- No designated leader: Leadership and participation are fully integrated. Each voice arises naturally in service of the group purpose.

- Unity and collective awareness: Participants experience themselves both as individuals and as a unified whole.

- Inherent connection: Connection is not something to "achieve"—it simply is. The group functions as a coherent intelligence.

- Spontaneous emergence: The process unfolds moment by moment, unrestricted by past patterns or structures.

- Expression without judgment: Each participant contributes freely and is received fully. All expressions are experienced as serving the greater whole.

- Creativity and originality: The group continually generates new ways of interacting, moving beyond duality and limitation.

- Experience of oneness: Participants feel deeply connected, expressing as and through the being of the group.

Examples of New Wave Groups and When They Are Effective

- Visionary think tanks: Groups that operate without hierarchy, allowing deep collective insight and innovative breakthroughs.

- Spiritual or meditation circles: Participants attune to a shared presence without needing guidance from a single leader.

- Advanced creative ensembles: Musicians, dancers, or artists who co-create without set direction, trusting emergence.

- Cutting-edge tech or design teams: Groups that operate as fluid, adaptive ecosystems where all members contribute equally.

- Transformational retreats: Gatherings where deep unity consciousness is prioritized, and structure dissolves in favor of presence.

- Highly evolved communities: Groups fully attuned to collective intelligence, living in deep coherence.

Benefits of New Wave Groups

- Collective intelligence and emergence allow the group to operate as a unified field of wisdom.

- Effortless flow and coherence enable interactions without force or external control.

- Unrestricted creativity allows participants to freely express themselves without judgment or hierarchy.

- Deep connection and unity provide an experience of being part of a larger, coherent whole.

- Spontaneous and transformational dynamics enable deep personal and collective evolution.

Conclusion

Groups evolve from structure to flow, from separation to unity, and from hierarchy to shared intelligence. While most groups move between these phases, recognizing where a group is on the Continuum allows for a greater awareness and intentionality in how we engage.

Each step along this Continuum offers a different way of relating, and the deeper we go, the more we move into the experience of effortless collaboration and open-hearted unity.

There is no formula, just the choice to be present, again and again. That's how groups evolve, and how we learn what's possible.

Qualities of a Self-Aware New Wave Group

This section goes more deeply into the lived experience of being a New Wave group. We use the term self-aware to describe moments when a group not only functions as a unified whole but also recognizes itself as such.

This vision may sound idealized, but it arises from experience—times when our own groups (i.e., gatherings of two or more) have cohered into something unmistakably alive and unified. We may touch into this awareness briefly—even fully arising as it—yet most of the time we move in and out of its qualities. It is not a fixed state but a living, ever-expanding possibility. A single glimpse leaves an imprint, a felt reminder of what is possible.

By giving voice to some of these experiences, our intention is to create a path to recognize their presence and aspire to this level of awareness. These descriptions offer a compass inviting us to move more consciously and intentionally toward unity.

Your tendency as the reader may be to quickly skim the list. We invite you to slow down. As you read each quality, bring yourself into sensing what it might feel like—in your body, your nervous system, and your heart.

Awareness of Itself as a Living Being

- The group senses itself as more than the sum of its parts.

- Members recognize they are arising as the group intelligence, not separate from it.

- There's an experiential recognition of the being of the group.

- Attunement to frequency and energetic coherence are continuous.

- The group maintains a high level of energetic clarity.

- There's collective sensitivity to shifts in tone, emotion, and presence.

- When frequency drops (i.e., tension, confusion, disconnection), the group notices and tends to it.

Presence and Spaciousness

- Silence is welcomed and valued.

- There is an unforced rhythm—space for intuition, emergence, and pause.

- Time isn't rushed, if experienced at all.

- Whatever is arising is fully honored.

Unified Intention and Purpose

- The group holds a shared, evolving intention that feels alive.

- Individuals are aligned with the group's deeper movement, rather than competing agendas.

- Purpose is articulated clearly but also held lightly, leaving room for emergence.

No Need for Expert Control

- Leadership is shared, flexible, and co-arising.

- Transparency and authenticity are natural.

- Every voice is valued, and there's trust in the group's innate intelligence.

Emotional and Relational Maturity

- Conflict is not avoided but approached with curiosity and heart.

- There's a baseline of emotional responsibility and self-awareness.

- Members don't collapse into projection, or blame—they are self-responsible.

Deep Listening and Mutual Seeing

- Everyone is deeply heard, beyond words.

- Listening includes the field.

- A sense of being profoundly met by the group is common.

Aliveness and Creative Flow

- Meetings feel energizing, surprising, and nourishing.

- Insight, humor, and synchronicity often arise spontaneously.

- There's joy in the collaboration—something greater is clearly at play.

- In a self-aware group, individual needs, longings, and intentions aren't ignored or overridden by the collective. Instead, they become essential threads in the unfolding intelligence of the group.

Individual Longings Are Invitations

- Personal longings often point to what the group itself is ready to open to.

- When someone brings a deep longing or intention, it activates something for the whole field.

- In a self-aware group, we listen for the group's longing as it arises through individuals.

- The individual doesn't get swallowed by the group—the group gets deepened by the individual.

Needs Are Honored, Not Managed

- Instead of fixing or bypassing needs, the group stays present with them.

- A need for rest, clarity, reassurance, or space is seen as a signpost, not a disruption.

- Attending to real needs in real time actually increases the coherence of the group.

Intentions Are Held Lightly but Powerfully

- Individual intentions are shared transparently and allowed to evolve.

- The group supports each member in clarifying their own true intention—not as a goal, but as an inner orientation.

- These personal intentions create resonance and help align the group's collective movement.

No One Has to Fragment to Belong

- You don't have to leave part of yourself at the door to participate.

- The group welcomes paradox—personal longing and group coherence can coexist.

- When individuals show up whole, the group field actually stabilizes and amplifies.

The Group Amplifies the Individual's Evolution

- The more coherent the group field, the more it uplifts and clarifies each person's journey.

- It's not about losing individuality—it's about amplifying your essence by the field of unity.

- You may feel more yourself in a self-aware group than even when you're alone.

- It's a truly holographic dance. The group reveals itself through you, and you reveal yourself through the group.

- A self-aware group doesn't just allow healing—it activates it. But not in the way we often think of healing as something linear, private, or requiring intervention. In the field of a self-aware group, healing is a natural consequence of presence, coherence, and unity.

The Field Itself Is Healing

- In a self-aware group, the field becomes so coherent and attuned that it naturally begins to reorganize what's fragmented or unresolved—without needing to "do" anything.

- This field holds the full continuum of what is—light and shadow, beauty and mess—without judgment.

- That deep, accepting presence is the healing.

- The group doesn't fix you. It holds you in a frequency where what needs to unwind can unwind, and what wants to emerge can emerge.

Healing Through Recognition

- Simply being seen—truly, non-reactively, without a label—is one of the most healing experiences a person can have.

- In a self-aware group, people feel recognized not just for their story or wounds, but for their essence.

- That kind of seeing restructures identity in real time. Old patterns lose their grip.

Mutuality and Belonging Heal Isolation

- So many wounds are about separation, shame, or "not being part of."

- A self-aware group offers a direct experience of belonging at the level of being—not for what you do, but for who you are.

- This rewires relational patterns, even those formed early in life.

Attunement and Safety Regulate the Nervous System

- The coherence and presence of a self-aware group entrain nervous systems into regulation.

- When a person who's dysregulated comes into a space where the frequency is high and clear, their system begins to shift without force.

- This embodied shift lays the groundwork for real healing—not just conceptual insight.

Wholeness Is Reflected, Not Fragmentation

- A self-aware group doesn't orient around problems or pathologies.

- It reflects the wholeness that's already present, even when someone is hurting.

- That reflection calls forward a deeper identity—the one beneath the pain.

Healing Happens in the We, Not Just the Me

- Sometimes, what arises in one person is felt by others in the group.

- The group may process or move something together, in shared silence, movement, or resonance.

- Healing, then, is not an individual event—it's a group revelation.

- In a self-aware group, healing is less about "working on" and more about "being with." Less about fixing, more about revealing. Less about the person, more about the field.

Eight Elements That Move Any Group Toward Unity Consciousness

Awareness and Acknowledgment of
Higher Intelligence

Opening the Heart by Nurturing a Unitive Perspective
(No Right, Wrong, or Judgment)

Attending to the Presence of Silence

Articulating Intention

Emergence / Letting Nature Lead

Non-Expert Model / Transparency

Co-Leadership Model / Self-Agency

Attending to Frequency / Connection

Eight Elements That Move Any Group Toward Unity Consciousness

Elements That Foster an Environment for Group Awakening

Awareness and Acknowledgment of Higher Intelligence

There are always successively higher orders of intelligence. Our "higher self;" the group field or being; Nature; spiritual teachers or guides; your muse; God; Great Spirit; numen; star beings; ancestors; Evolution. So many names for whatever we encounter when we expand out beyond our limiting egos and embrace the mystery.

In any conversation, there is a moment of choice to open to the simple awareness of higher intelligence, and then, we are open to knowing that we too are it.

Opening the Heart by Nurturing a Unitive Perspective (No Right, Wrong, or Judgment)

A position of neutrality, away from the hold of the ego's need for judgment and evaluation, enables the heart to wrap all beings and situations in love and wisdom.

Opening the heart heals any separation.

Attending to the Presence of Silence

There is a state of deep internal quiet. Stopping all speaking, sound, and perhaps movement and listening to the voice of silence. No expectation. No demand. No needing to know. Resting. Simply being.

> **In the deepest silence, I recognize the energy of my own journey. I hear the song of the universe and know my place in it. And I know you there also.**
>
> — *Anonymous*

192

Element That Brings the Group Being Into Coherence

Articulating Intention

A simple statement of why two or more are gathered highlights, attunes, aligns, and empowers the group purpose.

> There is nothing capricious in nature. The implanting of a desire indicates that its gratification is in the constitution of the creature who feels it.
> —Ralph Waldo Emerson

The Creative Force

Emergence / Letting Nature Lead

Emergence means following Nature's call in every moment, every situation. It is the natural and uninhibited arising of self.

Emergence is the creative moment at its purest.

> The mountains are calling and I must go.
> —John Muir

Elements That Enable the Optimal Flow-Through of Life Energy / Creativity

Non-Expert Model / Transparency
and its Corollary Element

Co-Leadership / Self-Agency
When we no longer place authority outside ourselves, the split between "leader" and "participant" dissolves.

No transference—just presence.

Each person is free to be fully themselves, and fully the group.

> **Our vitality and strength emerge when we release dependency on external leaders and find the courage to carve our own path.**
>
> —*J. Krishnamurti*

Group Maintenance and Hygiene

Attending to Frequency / Connection
Wherever we are, every time we raise our frequency by any amount, that next higher frequency has more...love, unity, coherence, information, complexity, possibility, freedom, creativity. Coherence means love, gratitude, peace. Those emotions are by definition coherent.

> **When a complex system is far from equilibrium, small islands of coherence in a sea of chaos have the capacity to shift the entire system to a higher order.**
>
> —*Ilya Prigogine*

Meet The Authors

Anne Altvater is the founder of Campbell's Lane Horse and Donkey Farm, Insight Equine Therapy, and Great Bear Retreat Venue. Her work brings together people, animals, and nature in a living partnership that opens pathways of healing and attunement. For decades she has welcomed individuals and groups into environments that are grounded, heart-centered, and alive with possibility. With a steady presence and a deep trust in the wisdom of relationship, human and more-than-human. Anne helps others soften into authenticity and discover new ways of connection and healing.

Patricia Pfost has spent more than four decades teaching, facilitating groups, and guiding others in personal and collective growth. Her work weaves familiar educational approaches with an awareness of the subtler dimensions of human connection, helping people discover deeper ways of relating to themselves and each other. As a somatic and energy therapist, she has supported individuals and groups through times of challenge and transition, always pointing toward greater self-agency and authentic presence. Patricia has a way of naming what matters with clarity and care. Her presence encourages us to step into what feels most genuine, alive, and meaningful.

Their shared curiosity drew them together: What allows a group, or even two people, to discover meaning, coherence, and presence that no one could find alone? And their collaboration continually gives rise to something larger than either of them—a shared work, a living field of awareness, and a model for groups as places of transformation.

Eight Elements That Move Any Group Toward Unity Consciousness

Awareness and Acknowledgment of Higher Intelligence

Opening the Heart by Nurturing a Unitive Perspective (No Right, Wrong, or Judgment)

Attending to the Presence of Silence

Articulating Intention

Emergence / Letting Nature Lead

Non-Expert Model / Transparency

Co-Leadership Model / Self-Agency

Attending to Frequency / Connection

This list is for you to cut out so you always have it on hand for a quick tangle reference.